I AM NOT AN INCONSEQUENTIAL

WORD

I faced soul killers on my journey
to womanhood, and I survived.

I AM NOT AN INCONSEQUENTIAL

WORD

POETRY & REMNANTS

JACALYN EYVONNE

ISBN 978-1-7354936-3-3 (Paperback Edition)
ISBN 978-1-7354936-4-0 (Hardcover Edition)

Cover Design & Images by NeuImagery
Published by JE Books
First Printing September 2022

Contact: www.JacalynEyvonne.com

To all those who think you can't,
But can!

CONTENTS

PREFACE

res·o·lute

adjective
   1. "She had the resolute to change her life and live."

Jacalyn Eyvonne

I Wasn't Always a Queen

I stumbled. I fell many times along the way to womanhood, questioning my value and self-worth. I let people define me and frequently allowed my skin color to hold me back. I often felt like I was prey to people who hated me and others pretending to love me. It was only through hit-and-miss that I was able to grow into the person I am.

As a child, my mom regularly recited 'sticks and stones.' I remember standing on the playground several times after being called black, ugly, or worse yet, the N-word, crying and repeating a retaliating response.

"Words can't hurt me! Words can't hurt me!"

Over time, I realized that my mother was wrong. Words can and do hurt, and they have hurt me badly.

I walked around in a superficial illusion for many years, behaving as though hurtful words bounced right off me— my way of attempting to survive the turmoil in my mind. I was trying to live up to being the better person, except I was a fake, and it wasn't working.

The church and my mom counseled me to ignore the hatred, reciting Matthew 5 verse 39 from the King James Version of the Bible.

"But I say unto you, That ye resist not evil: but whosoever shall smite thee on thy right cheek, turn to him the other also."

I was not to let words bother me but instead let this be my way of turning the other cheek to cruelty. I was programmed to let words go, not realizing that I was emotionally dejected. Unaware as a child that negative comments were seeping deep into my soul, concealed away in hidden spaces in my mind.

It wasn't until I became a mother that I realized the reality in which my skin lived was disparaged in my country since birth. I had battled against the feelings of being ugly or that something was wrong with me because of harsh words swarming around me all my life. Not feeling good about who I was, opened the door for other hurts to enter my life.

I came to grips with a society guilty of the stigmatization and reinforcement of negativity about black people in everything around me. For some, my life wrapped in melanin was a threat. That threat carried over to my children. The words that haunted me my entire life now circled back to my family. It wasn't about me any longer. It was beyond me.

I'll never forget the day my husband Frank had to jump-start the car battery. My inquisitive seven-year-old son Neuman was looking on in what became a teachable moment for Frank. Frank was proud to show Neuman how to connect the charging cables to the battery terminals.

"Always remember that the red is positive. See the plus sign? Black has a minus sign because it's negative."

However, the first question in response from Neuman was, "But Dad, why is black always negative?"

The question went right over Frank's head, and he responded, "It just is, and it's important always to remember that, or you can damage the car."

But I saw the confusion on my son's face. Neuman has always questioned everything. He has never accepted anything without asking why. So, after a moment of silence, Neuman continued.

"That's not what I mean, dad. Why is the color black always negative? We're black, so are we negative?"

That was the day I sat down and talked with my son. It was the beginning talk, unlike the talks that would come later. I explained the negative conditioning in society's use of words and symbolism of how white is appealing; white is good. In contrast, black describes evil, death, and mourning. I talked about the difference in a child growing up with words symbolic of skin colors, such as innocent, light, peace, cleanliness, faith, goodness, and redemption. White represents virginity in a wedding dress, purity, luck, or white as snow. The approved list is the 'white list,' and the noble hero is the 'white-knight.' The 'good witch' wears white, standing for freshness and clarity. Even a 'white lie' is not a big deal, while a 'white Christmas' is most desirable.

My son has always been an advanced thinker. He voiced his observations on the stark opposite references to the word black and its relation to despair, darkness, negativity, nightmares, dampened moods, and even pain.

Black is aggression, grief, mourning, sadness, and sin. 'Black magic' is bad magic. An outcast from society or family is the 'black sheep,' and illegal trade is the 'black market.' The 'black witch' is the evil witch.

I listened to my son and knew it was the right time to ensure he understood he was not mistaken. That it was instead society's mistake.

We also talked about turning the other cheek, sharing how I was impacted by allowing hurt feelings to reside within me. I wanted him to understand that ignorance thrives when we fail to correct the behavior of our abusers, not through violence but through education and discussion. An essential step to standing up and challenging hate is protecting yourself and your soul.

My son is now grown, and we continue to have deep conversations on issues of race, protecting oneself, and commanding respect.

I have lived through numerous references to who I am or what I am. Between the 1960s and late 1970s, with the emergence of the Black Power movement, I was in my teenagehood and all-in on calling myself black over negro. I found it empowering, a way of embracing my blackness. Nearing the latter part of the '80s, the term African American became popular, and I fully adopted that coinage. I wanted to know my connection to Africa, although I had no inkling about my lineage. My resentment at not having a link to my heritage began to explode.

WHO AM I?

I don't know
who the hell I am
apart from me

Who am I? Was the question,
I asked myself throughout my life.
I was my mom's daughter,
my birthright rooted in
The United States.
Even so, I questioned,
Who the hell I am
apart from me?
Words have labeled me
colored
negro
black
African
African American
and yes,
I've been called the N-word,
and other things depending upon
the name caller's inspiration.
Still, I needed to understand,
Who the hell I am
apart from me?

I had no ancestral family tree.
No lines of descent that I could
reach back into a story of my lineage
where I could draw from strength.
I was desperate for that connection,
a sense of my dynasty.
I cannot say to you that I'm
South African
Kenyan
Tanzanian
or Watusi
I'm unable to tell you who
my ancestors were. Nigerian
Ethiopian
or Somalian?
Because I have no knowledge about
Who the hell I am,
apart from me.
My mother's mother passed on the birthing
table, thrusting her into existence.
Her father, my grandfather, died when
mom was 16, only a child herself.
Left without stories to share with me
because she had no clue.
Who the hell she was, apart from herself,

leaving me with no answers because
she had none to give.
Even though I asked and asked.
My passage through life was difficult
devoid of history, a non-being without
reminders of myself.
There was no birth father in my life.
No grandparents, no sager of wisdom
to share experiences of their past.
Unknowing leaves you soaked in emptiness,
open only to the imagination, dreaming
where my greatness might lie, musing
about the forefathers that may have breathed
life throughout my veins, instilling
the courage of resilience, the backbone
I would need in life to propel me through
a world where I am judged by words.

I don't know
Who the hell I am,
apart from me.
But I can tell you this.
There is a specialness
in me, and I am listening.

After my mother passed in 2016, I ordered heritage tests for myself. I went with two companies to compare and see how close they were. To my surprise, the numbers were quite similar, 84% Sub-Saharan African, predominantly Nigerian, with Sierra Leonean being my second highest percentage. I have wondered my entire life about my history, and now I have a place of reference, and it feels good.

I have faced racism from teachers, on the street, in job interviews, on the job, and from medical providers. But I endured the negatives of being a woman, the restrictions and double standards rooted in gender biases. Being weak, unpromotable, and easily labeled a whore for having too many sexual partners. And, as a black woman, I weathered the hallmark attached to my skin color of being too angry, too bossy.

So, when my daughter was born in 1969, she became my princess. I told her how beautiful and pretty she was. We would look into the mirror together, and I would point out her features, telling her how cute her nose was and how lovely her lips were. I told her that her skin was ebony, royal, and majestic. She grew up believing in herself, loving herself, in her power. She never thought that she needed to change herself physically for acceptance by anyone. I taught her self-love. She is a Queen today, as is any woman I meet and respect. Women with wisdom who love and respect themselves as they do others, no matter their color. They are my Queens.

I still interchange the use of the words Black or African American today. I embrace both terms for myself, taking the word black and wearing it as a positive. Equally, taking the word 'Queen' and applying it to my sisters has become even more empowering.

I have fought hard all my life. I've fought for my family, love, respect, and justice. As a woman, specifically a black woman, my daily burden includes fighting for acceptance. Recognition that I am equal and that my family and I are simply allowed to live.

I have become a warrior in my own right. And, over the years, I have become more than proud. My Afrikan ancestry is the blood that flows through my ancestral line, where kings and queens were heads of villages.

I understand that the United States is not a monarchy, which has nothing to do with it. As I have heard espoused, it has nothing to do with a lack of self-esteem or an inferiority complex.

Instead, I tell America and the world that I am essential through my inherent anointing. I don't need anyone's approval to know how important I am. Today, I can dismiss a society that continually stereotypes and degrades me.

I accept the beauty
in my features
and my natural hair.
I welcome my melanin,
no matter what the shade or hue.
I love myself. I own my Blackness.
I am resolute
in my determination.
It is called pride.

Mother, Queen

The memories swell, exploding inside me
the love, the misunderstandings,
the sadness.
Did I apologize enough,
Did I tell her I loved her before she fell ill?
I wonder if she heard my words
the ones whispered in her ear,
as she lay still and quiet
days before taking her last breath.

My mother died this year.
I celebrate the miracles of her body,
The birther of my life, the giver of me
my creator, my Mother, my Queen.

My heart breaks,
my mind explodes,
obsessed with the memories.
The hurt/her tears.
Was I too hard on my momma?
Was I unfair?
To the woman who went to lengths
to keep me clothed,
who endured life's hardships to nourish me?
The possessor of life's greatest gift
The life she gave to me.

No man can come close to what
my Mother, my Queen, could do/did.

I want to shout from the hilltops,
scream to the heavens.
I love you, Mother, Queen.
I may not have said it enough, but I do.
I love you. I hope you can hear me now.

Purple Cloud

A purple cloud of natural splendor
clustered in emotions, blossoming
in the embrace of life.
Her beguiling beauty
resilient to the harsh winds
of her existence.
Generous when drenched in
liquid love/addictive/like honey
fueled by warmth
radiating from the sun.
A cherished enchantment
the flowering of beauty/that reigns
from season to season.
Flowing in the glory of
her history/of the bountiful
African Cape.
She is the royal flower of
hope and love.

I Dream of Wakanda

A magnificently beautiful land where I am
a descendant of kings and queens,
a land of great wealth,
a land of nobility.
The warm blood of Sub-Saharan Africa
runs through me,
Nigeria, Sierra Leonean, West African pride.
Birth from a glorious ancestry,
an heir of prideful, strong,
and determined people.
I am an African,

I dream of my homeland, my people.
Those who remain,
and those who crossed the vast,
distant sea, hearing the cries
of souls immersed in chilled waters
buried in the oceanic abyss.
I stand with the enduring anguish
of the torments of slavery,
and intense suffering. Spilling tears
over the merciless deaths at the hands
of those in quest of a new homeland.
Forcing their way of life on my people.
I am an American.

I am heir to two continents,
separated only by a vast sea,
bound together by the souls that
exist in my spirit, the spirit of
both people.
I feel the kinship.
The longing to know more has always
been a part of me.
My heritage calls out,
surging through every part of
my being, breathing into my heart,
conveying the ceremonial rites, my passage.
My consciousness dances,
knowing the nobility
that engulfs my awakening.
The power of who I
am flows through my veins.

I dream of Wakanda,
a magnificent kingdom filled with
wisdom and the spirit of determination,
surrounded by mountain ranges
and sprawling jungles because that is all
that I require to remind me of my greatness.
I am proud of my legacy, imagined or real.
I am an African American.

I Am Not An Inconsequential Word

Jacalyn Eyvonne

Chapter *1*

moth·er

noun

1. "When I looked into the mirror, my mother looked back at me, startling me at the close resemblance."

Jacalyn Eyvonne

Have I Turned Into You?

Oh my Gawd, I thought to myself, looking in the mirror, my eyes nearly touching the reflection. I looked like her, stood like her, moved like her, and sounded like her. What peered back at me was unsettling. I never wanted to be my mother.

My mother cleaned the homes of white people when I was an infant, leaving me with a sitter while she worked. Her smile sparkled as she talked about picking me up each night, poking my nose, and kissing my tiny lips. She told me how distant and angry I was in my babyish way, chuckling at my wrinkled forehead and scrunched frown, looking like anger. But believing my belly was about to fart out a few gas bubbles.

Sadness replaced her smile quite suddenly. I can still hear her voice, quietly speaking off into the distance to herself, looking away from me. If as though asking a question of herself.

"There was a sadness in your eyes, but you couldn't have been that angry? You were too little."

I loved my mother dearly, but our closeness faded as the moon circled the sun over the passing years. I was angry at her as a young girl. I became rebellious, mad at her for things she did or things I felt she didn't do when she should have. I was in a place where it took me a long time to forgive. I moved past much of my anger at my mother. Understanding that she likely felt much of the fear I felt growing into my womanliness.

I often wonder if that feeling of sadness ever left me, what she saw in my eyes or what I saw in hers. Curious about what might have happened while she was away—not understanding how an infant could feel such profound sadness or anger. Later, understanding how sorrow can find its way to vacillate inside you for many years.

I birth my daughter into the world at an early age. A few years later, I still practiced motherhood, raising my daughter and a beautiful white-haired Afghan Hound. Not knowing what I was doing but trying my best, I now had a daughter and a dog named Cognac. My favorite drink at the time. Now rearing my daughter and a dog, we clumped together in a tiny one-bedroom apartment in Los Angeles.

My heart raced after finding the rent increase notice slipped under the door. Frantic, I could no longer afford to pay. Only 60 days to find another place to live. I searched for another apartment that would accept a small child and my favorite, Cognac. There were none. My choice, though painful, was not difficult.

I sought a family to adopt Cognac. I felt like I was giving up one of my limbs. We were all three so close. Cognac was a big part of our family; I would miss that connection to my favorite drink.

After Cognac was adopted, my daughter and I settled into our new, tiny one-bedroom apartment.

More moons later, I saw a woman walking a beautiful white Afghan Hound down the street. I didn't recognize the woman, but I immediately recognized Cognac.

I yelled out from across the street and darted over to him. When he saw me, he leaped into the air with excitement. As I kneeled to pet him, his demeanor sharply changed. He abruptly jerked his head from me and became staunchly still. I continued to pet him, yet he remained distant. He no longer acknowledged my presence.

Seconds later, the woman gently pulled him away and continued down the street. I had abandoned him. And, though his first response was excitement, he soon realized he could not forgive me. I can still feel the hurt in my gut when I think about him. I understood at that moment the emotional toll the feeling of abandonment could have on someone or something: an infant child or even a pet. I never saw him again and no longer drink cognac.

Was this what I felt when I was an infant, each day my mother left me for hours with a stranger? I wondered what may have happened to me while she was away. Why did my eyes leave my mom filled with such sadness? Was there something inside me all these years that created the emotional distance I have always felt from my mother?

Moving through life awakens memories that resemble things mimicked in your presence. Watching the growing aggression on social media and TV reminds me of when I left my son at 14 months old with a childcare provider in Los Angeles.

The interview with the stocky, sandy-haired lady went quite well. She was religious. The big cross on the wall gave her away. Her smile was pleasant as she chuckled like a bird, giving me a tour of her home. I saw the other children in her care. She was nearby, and the price was something I could afford. After signing the daycare contract, my son was soon left under the charge of a white woman who laughed with a high-pitched whistle.

Things were going well for weeks; however, my husband and I noticed our son's temperament changed. He cried more often, and it seemed to worsen over the weeks.

I took my son to the doctor. He was healthy, though not

gaining weight as he should.

One day, I went to drop him off at the daycare, and when the woman opened the door, my son began screaming and clinging to me. The cries were not like anything I had ever heard from him before. As the daycare owner reached toward him, his screams grew louder while clinging aggressively to me. I looked at my son before looking back at her; she looked at me as we looked at each other, and I said, "I won't be leaving him with you today after all."

Reflections of my mother visited me that day. What I saw in my son's frightened eyes, desperately clinging to me, made me wonder if that was the voiceless sadness my mother saw in me as an infant. Had I betrayed my son the same way I may have been as an infant? Leaving him with a stranger. A stranger who may have hurt or abused him?

I imagined everything negative that may have happened to him in her company. I questioned why I didn't see the abuse that might have been occurring. Why didn't my mother?

Something happened to my son during his daycare stay. He was too young to speak of his experience. His eyes and his actions told me all I needed. I do not doubt that what I am saying is true. That was the last time Neuman stayed at a daycare. I stopped working. I became a stay-at-home mom. This put all the burden of income generation on my husband, who, I must add, struggled at putting food on the table.

Why agree to watch my child only to abuse him? Why accept money from someone you despise?

The longstanding disdain for black people in this country is nothing new. My mother experienced it. I still experience it. I don't know if my son's mistreatment was due to his black skin or if the sitter was simply unbalanced. You can't trust a cross on the wall and her bird-like whistle offered no clue.

The daycare provider's mask was exposed that day. Her façade was superficial. She presented an illusion of something she was not. In the same way, true feelings about black people are revealed by those removing their masks of racism today.

Unspoken Bias

Faces hide the mask of hate, but not forever.
Arrogance is always uncovered.
Your privilege screams loudly at me
rising through the sweat on your brow
when you become nervous
when you feel challenged
on your right to abuse others.
That self-imposed right to feel superior to
those whose hue is darker than yours.

The mask shields the hate for a moment
revealing itself through your words
and actions over time,
subtle messages, moods, demeanor,
that expression on your face
when faced with challenges
that you don't like.

Societal changes frighten you
"More black and brown people coming.
Too many of their babies being born."
Close the borders, don't let them in.
Overrun by the
black as night takeover.
The mask reveals itself over time
You can't hide your hate forever.

It's the little actions, the small words
that tells us who you are.

That privilege you believe
to be owed to you.
Thinking you are better than
you are,
Thinking you are
better than me.

I saw it today
the mask once again revealed
when I placed my green dollars
into your anxious palm, yet
when I held my black hand out
to receive my change,
you flung it on the counter.

You don't have to speak the words,
"I don't like you."
You show me daily
by the petty things you do.

Molding/The Kiln of Life

Hands press and glide across the surface
of a new life.
Rolling and shaping with gentle touches
like a clay mold spinning
on a potter's wheel.
Crafting lines of words, thoughts
and emotions,
pitching and smoothing daily
towards the future.
Instilling a sense of purpose
while tempered and glazed,
in the heat of the kiln.

Hands lay out the canvas of a child's life.
Be careful in your crafting
support and mold growth toward
tenacity and purpose,
without cracking or overheating.
Careful not to soak up the excess of your past,
spilling it over into the future.
Guide and build the lines and patterns,
add a sturdy base, a steppingstone
that instills purpose and beauty.

Steady the pace on the wheel,
as the new life gains strength

To become centered.
Build up the walls slowly,
with the will to conquer.

Take heed as you form
the shape of tomorrow.

Sleep Tight

"I'm tired," she'd say.
Grabbing the side of her hip
as though it would ease
the pain of aging over wearying years.
"It's 7:00 am. Don't be late for school."
Repeating the words daily after arriving home
from her overnight graveyard shift,
where she caressed the premature babies
of other mothers—holding them close to her heart
as if holding her own.
I've never known a day when my mother
didn't work or didn't hold babies.
She loved her preterm little ones.
Sharing her joys with these tiny souls,
and her anguish over some not having
the time to grow to avoid the problems,
praying for their survival.

"Hurry and get ready," she'd say.
Retelling how she didn't get a chance
to finish school. How she struggled, learning
to read and write on her own.
"Be thankful for the opportunities you have,"
she'd say, passing down her wise words
and lessons learned.
"I'll be leaving soon," I'd say.

Her wearied face still hides her actual age.
The joy and sadness.

I hope I look like her when I'm that age.
I'd often think to myself.
My momma was a pretty woman,
the remnants of beauty still present
beyond the lines on her face.
"I'm on my way to bed now. Don't be late."
"I won't," I say.
"Sleep tight."

Jacalyn Eyvonne

Chapter 2

yes·ter·year

noun

    1. "It is my yesteryear to choose to remember or forget."

Jacalyn Eyvonne

In The Old Days

At the first flicker of the streetlamps, I bounded toward the house, my younger sister behind me. Our friends scurried off to their own homes as our youthful voices resonated one after another, converging slowly over the darkening sky.

"Bye, see you tomorrow."

Knowing, without question or hesitation, the rule was a simple one. At the flicker of those lights, head towards home. Only seconds to get through the door. The light was our warning, and mom would be waiting at the entrance.

Life was uncomplicated. We roller-skated and shared turns riding bikes, hula-hooped, and dodged balls while enjoying hide-and-go-seek, tag, and hopscotch.

We jumped into and ran through water sprinklers on hot days, soaking ourselves in cool falling droplets. Never thinking twice about lips drenched in the water spilling from the hose. Sharing the flowing stream between giggles. We stopped playing, only to enjoy sips from a tall plastic cup of lemonade or a slice of cantaloupe. Those were fun times.

It was even better on the weekends. Neighbors sat on porches; others locked horns over games of bid-whiz on front lawns. Only stopping for lunch and dinner from our endless fun. We'd lie on our backs in the grass to further entertain ourselves, delighting at the fanciful, dreamlike cloud formations. We'd count the first stars in the distant sky as the evening twilight crept in.

It could be as late as nine pm when the lamps signaled the time for us to stop our play. Until that moment, we were full of laughter. Those were periods of carefree innocence. Days that I will never forget.

We lived on 104th Street in Los Angeles. I was eight years old. My little sis was six. By this point, my mother had married my stepfather. We had our own house, a big yard, and a fenced-in backyard. Mom's marriage had upgraded our living standards from the project housing. It was a new life for the family. We also welcomed a new companion, Pepper, a beautiful black and white cocker spaniel. Our very first dog.

We were euphoric in this new way of life.

Deja Vu

Momma's fried chicken and pork ribs
filled the entire neighborhood
with aromatic smells
that had to leave the neighbors jealous.
When I was young, I leaned more towards
the hot dogs and mac and cheese.
At twelve, I developed a taste
for the grown people spread,
which also included mashed tatters
and gravy, collard/turnip greens,
cornbread and corn on the cob.
I had another reason for gravitating
to more than the hot dogs.
I wanted to appear older
to the grownups, sipping hard liquor
and gossiping in the backyard.
Still, young enough to laugh
through lips covered in a thick
Texas-styled sauce, while
chasing my cousins with sticky fingers.
My mother was born in Texas.

Card tables with folding chairs filled
the yard and covered patio,
other family members and guest
remained indoors, away from the

sun's heat, seated on the couches
and chairs covered in plastic,
likely causing a bit of butt sweat
on sweltering hot days.
Momma rarely turned on the
air-conditioner, not even for guests.
We/drenched in sweat
during the summer. Our buns
freezing cold in the winter.
She didn't believe in
paying high gas bills,
regardless of how chilly or
humid it was. Mom would say
"If you that cold, go put on
some socks and a sweater."
As the music played, loud talking
men showed off and showed out over
card games, an occasional woman
joining them.

Mom was a soft-spoken shy woman
who tried hard at conversation,
but she tended her guests well
making sure she met their needs,
and refilling their red plastic cups
with more liquor.

My momma's shyness also exists in me.
It shows itself often
when I'm around people.
Now and then, I would sneak a sip
from a cup, giggling at my wooziness
from the nasty tasting brew.
Still sipping, like the pretty lady
in the red shirt that always showed up.
Her hair/immaculate
the perfect size body and
a burst of laughter that captured
everyone's attention, including mine.

I learned to cook better than
my momma ever could, but she
was the one that got me started.
I still see her smile, that awkwardness,
the shyness I inherited.
I can still smell the barbecue
grilling in the backyard
surrounded by loud laughter and love.
Reminded every time I cook,
every time I barbecue,
every time I wear my red shirt.

The Albatross

I didn't learn how to swim
until I became an adult.
Reminded of the day
of my near drowning,
captured by the might
of a sudden wave,
swallowing me whole
sucking my breath away
as I sank/flailed in slow motion.
Fearful that the end of my story
was near.
Saved by a nearby swimmer
choking/gasping/vomiting away
salty water from my chest and airways.

Water became my albatross,
an inescapable burden
of disasters followed.
Sewage water from the city
where unkept water pipes caused
flooding of my Berkeley office.
My daughter fell off a boat.
Struck by lightning,
on a hilltop holding an umbrella
foolishly in a rainstorm
at a campground surrounded

by a bunch of cub scouts.
Wondering what I did to trigger
the anger of the albatross.

Yet, still drawn/fixated by
the never-ending waters
gazing out over the seas
mightiness for hours.

The ocean humbles you.
Its fury is to be respected.
Its power embraced
as the winds howl,
lashing across its surface,
or dances in rhythmic patterns.
Layers of sand hug my toes while
taking baby steps towards the waters.
Small waves break and ebb
along the shore, as I accept me
gaining new respect and appreciation
celebrating its mightiness,
transforming me, drawing me,
further from my fears.

Say Cheese

My two pigtails stood straight out from
the sides of hair parted down the middle,
stretched and pulled flat against my scalp.
Tightly bound inside loops
of rubber bands, forming puffs clenched
between greased edges of my wooly crown
before grown-up fingers carefully molded
my rigid braided plaits. The newly formed
pigtails hurt a little as they tugged against
my scalp, but the delight at feeling cute
eased the pain.

The bumblebee barrettes affixed
near the ends of the pigtails, added a
fanciful touch while weighting the braids
pulling them in a downward appearance,
no more Pippi cartoonish plaits.
The bee hair clips matched my stiff,
starched bee embroidered blouse
complimenting me and prettying me up.

I stood in the mirror that morning, every
chance I got, practicing my smile
before leaving the house, preparing for
the fleeting moment of a memory captured.
The entire class was excited about 'Picture Day!'

Soon a big cheesy smile stretched ear-to-ear
across my face. Grinning as the flash from
the traveling cameraman splashed a
bright light across the surface of me
forever remembered in that time and space.

Moon Magic

I couldn't sleep
In the silence
nearing midnight
that Christmas Eve.
Bustling with anticipation
for the arrival of
the first light
in the morning.
A family of three.
I shared a bedroom
with my sister.
Mom's bed was the couch.
We had no chimney.
We left no cookies
beneath our small
tabletop foil needled
Christmas tree.
We were poor project kids
before mom married
our stepdad.
I didn't realize
how poor we were
I was too happy.
Mom often made
our gifts.
Nothing close to what

the neighborhood kids
bragged about, yet
it was an enchanting time
for my sister and me.

That night was special
wide awake, glancing up
into the sky
I saw Santa and his sleigh,
reindeers at the helm
dashing past the moon.
Wide-eyed stare/focused
on the vivid sight before me.
Breathless/amazed/speechless
my gaping mouth prevented
words from escaping.
Overflowing with excitement
watching/staring in awe
until the sleigh
was out of sight
straining as it disappeared,
into the distance.
That morning/we tore open
our meticulously wrapped gifts
with a frenzy.

Three for me.
Three for my sister.
All handmade.
Then/mom surprised us
with two unique gifts
store-bought dolls,
our first real dolls
one for each of us.
I blurted out that Santa
left them/sharing
how I watched him overhead
passing in front of the moon.
Momma said it was
my imagination, that
it was just a dream.

I now know that Santa
doesn't exist, but I saw
something in the sky
that night/right before
midnight/when I was
a little girl, leaving a
bit of magic under the tree
and in my heart.

Flying High

His hand extended in my direction
It was my first gift from a boy
on a midsummer day.
Side by side on the playground swings
two lollipops, one cherry red
the other lemony yellow.
He let me choose.
I picked cherry red.
He didn't know that lollipops
were my favorite candy on a stick.
Smiling in his direction, he in mine.
Letting out a girly chuckle
as we encouraged each other's
nervousness over noisy laughter
from playful children
in the background.

Soon gliding back and forth
in rhythmic synch
moving in timed leans
pumping ourselves
towards the sky.
Hands gripping thick chain ropes,
Lips wrapped tightly around
the lollipops in our mouths.

Two eleven-year-olds
being young together
swinging against the wind
jumping at the precise moment.

I Am Not An Inconsequential Word

Jacalyn Eyvonne

Chapter 3

dis·hon·est

adjective

1. "It was as though my tongue had a life of its own; its dishonesty was outside my control."

Jacalyn Eyvonne

Your Nose Is Growing

I lost my way for a moment, traveling down the wrong path. The road swallowed me up quickly, digging its claws deep into my flesh as I walked along. I could hear myself crying while feeding on my guilt after my mistake.

When I was nine years old, my bad thing happened after my mom married my stepfather. We were poor before my mother married Alvin. Everything changed after they met.

Alvin worked for the post office but also cleaned businesses at night. He made an excellent income between both jobs.

Alvin invited me to work and help him clean the offices after hours. My first time earning an allowance, a shiny half dollar. Fifty cents was a lot of money for an eight-year-old.

Our new way of life seemed dreamlike. I never received an allowance before my mom married. The only coins that came to me were the nickels, dimes, or pennies I stumbled upon on the streets. I delighted in making my polished half-dollar each week.

After hours, we cleaned the offices, where I mostly emptied the trash and dusted. This one night, I spotted a bright red 1959 convertible Buick Electra model automobile sitting atop a desk. I'd never seen a toy car so polished-looking and beautiful.

My sister and I now owned a few store-bought dolls by this time, instead of the coke bottle dolly with mop hair mom used to make for us. We drove our toy dolls around in shoe boxes fastened atop metal roller skates.

The car was beguiling. The overhead light twinkled off the

bumper. I could see myself pushing my doll in it, rolling it across the bedroom floor. Before I knew it, it lay gripped inside my hand and found its way beneath my coat.

The following day, Alvin and my mom called me into the kitchen. When I sat in the chair opposite them, I dripped in fear, realizing my actions were ready to be exposed.

The workplace had phoned. The car, a red 1:18 scale die-cast replica, was missing from an employee's desk. He asked if I had taken it, and I quickly blurted out, "No."

I envisioned the story of Pinocchio. My nose tingled and itched. If they stared at me too closely, I believed they would see it move.

I glanced down toward the floor, unable to look at either of my parents. I bawled when Alvin asked me again if I'd taken the car.

"Yes," I said through wails and tears.

Mom ordered me to get the car, and I did, further stating how disappointed she was with me. I bawled even louder.

Alvin drove me to the office later that day. I'd never visited the building during daylight, and I felt the eyes behind every desk were all on me. We stopped in front of a white man seated behind a desk. His big, stern face stared down at me.

Alvin handed me the car and instructed me to apologize to him. My slight frame shook as I turned over the bright red model car to the older man whose eyes pierced through me.

"Sorry."

"Speak up," my stepfather said.

"Sorry," I repeated.

This turned out to be a terrifying time in my youthful life. Some say you shouldn't force a child to apologize. In my case, those people are wrong.

Alvin did not lose his cleaning job; he continued to service that business. I didn't collect the shiny half-dollar anymore; that being the last day I went to work with him. Likewise, it was the last time I took anything that didn't belong to me.

Source of Pain

The discomfort is different
when you're the cause
of someone's heartache.
An unsettling gloominess
burrows itself deep inside you,
wounding you in infinite ways.
Looking into the eyes of the
sadness executed by you
watching the disquieting sorrow,
the letdown and tears
rolling down a rattled face.
Weeping along with them
"I'm sorry," going unnoticed
when words fall short
against unbearable pain.

Beware the lure of shiny things

That gleam and smile back at you and
speak sweet words of entrapment,
into your ear. Bright sparkles
of enticement/slipping in/out
of your life/filling you
with the confidence/of getting
away with wrongdoings.
Lures attracting you away
from the ability to decide
right from wrong, leading you towards
the path into darkness.
Be careful of wrong choices
that can bring you to your knees.
The shiny things/promises
of something better/can lead you
to do the thing that makes things worse.

Look away/pullback
from the bedazzling deceptions
appearances of promise/quick cash
fast wealth/free stuff/that never
belong to you. The polished surfaces
radiate like whitened teeth,
or small shining disks of cheap plastic

sequin beaded across a pointy bra,
ugly/yet tempting.

Beware the lure of shiny things
evil is busier than you think
seeking ways to
cycle back to you.

Rancor reaches out to you, enticing
the lustful desires that could be
that which causes your life to fall apart.

The Day He Changed

There came a day
that changed my stepfather
from the teaching dad
who offered lessons learned,
and better choices.
Still, a skinny, flat-chested
little girl only a hair taller
just passing the 10-year-old-mark.
Too young, too naïve
to see it coming.
When hugs and kisses
turned into touches
between my legs
accompanied by two shiny
quarters and a whisper
"This is our special secret,
don't tell your mother."
His underestimation of my tiny frame,
and youthful resolve.

I handed the quarters to my mother
as soon as she walked through
the door. Telling on him!
Showing her how his hands crept.
Me stopping him
before he could take it further.

That day I told on the hands
that traveled between
my little girl legs.

Mom packed two suitcases
of belongings for the three of us,
mom, my sister, and me
before we left the house, believing
we were cutting ties for good.
Leaving behind my stepfather
to contemplate in shame.
The departure only lasted
for a few short weeks.
As woeful tears from
touchy-feely hands swayed
her to return to the place
where she forgave his traveling hands.
The day I changed and became
an angry, defiant black sheep.

Wondering if that shiny car
might have been my salvation.

Broken

In an instant, bonds that unite a family can
collapse and fall away. When grave mistakes
create heartbreak, leaving no space for going
back to what existed before.
Memories of joy replaced with
tearful footprints and trailing pain
following the incident
that caused the withering
of family dynamics.
Changing your life forever.

Momma Wasn't Always Okay

Momma was old school
in her beliefs/her mannerisms.
She spoke little about herself/her feelings.
Soft-spoken, her answer most often to the question
"Are you alright?" was "I'm okay,"
even when she wasn't.
When problems arose, momma would pray.
Praying meant she didn't have to address
the situation.
"God would handle it!" she'd say.
Believing the problem would fly away.

I believe momma wanted the best for us,
feeling she couldn't do it alone.
She didn't want to go backward to the projects
to the poverty where she worked so hard alone.
I believe momma loved me, loved us.
My sister and I. Yet I struggled to understand
how she would place me back
under the roof of such a calculating man,
the one who sought to harm me.
Whose disposition oozed with disdain
after the day of our return to his home,
becoming a child facing his vengefulness
because I was the child that told.

I would catch momma crying when alone.
It wasn't easy to miss her tear-stained eyes.
Still, I would ask, "Are you alright?"
and she would once again reply, "Oh, I'm okay."
That old-school part of her never saying why.

Watch Your Mouth

I cursed worse than an
ill-mannered man
out of earshot of those
threatening to wash my mouth
out with soap, when
I was fourteen.
Dropping word bombs
that I learned from others.
Hostile to those things
out of my control.
My nasty words
replaced my tears.
A way to hit back without
striking physical blows.
Entertained by the startled
gasps of surprise and "Oh No's!"
When I didn't want to be ladylike,
I drew pleasure in being
rude and foul-mouthed.

The Missile Toe Shoes

There was something mystical
about momma's shoes.
Not in the manner
in which she strolled
across the room, but more
the way they would follow me
when I oozed disrespect
mouthing off/talking back.
Until the shoe would come
off her foot/the point when
I took flight and ran.

Momma hurling her shoe
like a missile fired in my direction
she, livid at my audacity.
Me trying to get away
from the shoe's trajectory
as it passed through the
angry spaces in our home,
sprinting to outpace the shoe
following close behind me.
Believing there was safety
around the corner.

All I had to do was make it there.
But each time, that darn shoe
followed me around the bend,
striking me upside my head.
Wondering if her shoes
held some magical spell.

From the Heart

In dark hours, I listen to the drumming
of my heart as it breaks silence
and speaks.
Murmuring to me within the silent
spaces of time/when shadows
of pitch-black midnights besiege me,
and the storylines of existence
outside of my room sleeps within
the quiet background of night.
My ear pressed rigid against
the pillow/still of movement
following the sound of each pulse
over my unlabored breaths.
Fixated on the message
my heart was seeking to convey to me.
It is this minute before
lucid dreaming begins.
When rhythmic lub-dubs pulsate/
surge/and gallop louder/louder/
thundering inside me.
I listen.

Jacalyn Eyvonne

Chapter 4

preg·nant

adjective

1. "It was when I was pregnant in my seventh month that my belly began to sing to me."

Jacalyn Eyvonne

A State of Panic

The bulge in my stomach showed when my mother asked me if I was pregnant. My secret was now exposed by her one question. Raw panic caused me to rush to the bathroom, where I threw up violently.

Everything changed in early 1969. In my final year of high school, I realized a life lived in my belly.

I was a naïve 17-year-old, foolishly keeping a secret with no plan and an embarrassment to myself and my family. Worse yet, being pregnant and unwed in my upper-middle-class household meant I could no longer remain at home. At least, not while my belly became more prominent.

My mother and stepfather jointly agreed to place me under the charge of the Nuns at St. Anne's Maternity Home for Unwed Mothers.

The Franciscan Sisters of the Sacred Heart Catholic ministry greeted me, where I met girls ages 13 to 18—all unwed and of all races. White, Asian, or Black, we were all treated the same. I don't recall feeling discriminated against any more than the other girls. We were all imprisoned under the charge of Catholic Nuns, even if we weren't Catholic, and I wasn't. We were stuck there until we gave birth.

The Nuns were nothing like the stern-faced women in movies wielding wooden paddles or rulers. They were friendly, counseling us girls on mothering techniques and childbirth, even placing the child up for adoption.

The goal was to help me understand my options, make better choices, and turn me into a better person. However, I struggled with the adoption discussions. I was uncertain and felt pressured. Both mom and Alvin wanted me to give the baby up for adoption, but I didn't know what I wanted to do. Several girls ended up giving away their babies.

My best friend at St. Anne's was a Chinese girl. I'll call her Daiyu, though that is not her real name. I won't share her actual name because the birth may be a part of her unspoken past, as it is for many girls. And if I have to make up a name, Daiyu, which means black jade reminds me of her because she was my Chinese soul sister. She did not care about my skin color.

Daiyu and I developed an unusual closeness over the five months we boarded together. We were close in our terms of pregnancy, and we were also quite naughty together. We made a point of having fun and raising hell—our way of taking revenge on our forced environment in any way we could. We were both seventeen years old and trapped in the same situation.

We rebelled against the snotty girls who thought they were better than us, even finding themselves in the same situation.

I'll never forget when we dug up worms from the wet grounds around the facility after the rain or collected rocks and sneaked them into the beds of those loud mouths that we didn't like.

We took a blood oath. Daiyu slipped a knife from the cafeteria. We slit the tips of our index fingers and pressed them together, swearing our eternal friendship. We were blood sisters.

Daiyu was the first to give birth. She had signed her adoption papers two months earlier. The baby boy was at once removed and taken away. She cried all night.

The following day, her parents arrived to pick her up, and she introduced me to them. I could see the disapproving looks on their faces. Not only was I black, but I was also a pregnant unwed black, which made me even worse than their daughter, who found herself in the same situation as me. She was better than me at that moment. I could see it in their eyes.

I never saw Daiyu again after that day. Three weeks later, I gave birth to a seven-pound baby girl. I did not sign the adoption papers. My daughter, Nicole, came home with me. Alvin was unhappy, but when mom saw Nicole, her eyes lit up, and adoption discussions were over.

When I look back on it, the entire situation is quite laughable and somewhat sad at the same time. I could not stay home while my belly grew, but I was back home with a baby several months later. Go figure!

After settling back home in September 1969, I had a baby girl to take care of and multiple tough decisions ahead. I had just turned eighteen. Having continued my studies at St. Anne's, I had graduated high school on paper the prior June, receiving my diploma. I missed my senior prom and graduation ceremonies, which at that point, mattered little. Faced with my new title, mother, I had no clue where to begin. I grabbed a napkin and wrote my only single-word untitled poem: "Fuck!"

Amniotic Sea

Suspended in the sea of
my mother's womb
comforted by her whispers
of love,
and hands
pressed against the surface
of her stomach, reassured by
my movements.
My poking feet give her solace.
Amniotic fluids surround
the building blocks of life that protect.
My tiny body absorbs the
surroundings that sustain me.
Waiting to be dropped
into my new life.

Reflections

Overhead. A dim light,
hangs mid-ceiling.
Nighttime at St. Anne's.
The buzz of animated whispers
float across the room of bodies
spread across twin-sized beds.
Murmurings so the Nuns won't hear
us past the bedtime hour.
Big belly roommates
awaiting their turn to deliver
flocked closely,
in the maternity home
a place for unwed girl mothers.

Chitchat and gossip
about how they became pregnant,
whether they hope for a boy or a girl.
"I'm giving mine away,"
a 14-year-old sighs.
"Me too," chimes in the backdrop.
A room filled with little girls and
not so ready young ladies, amid
immature giggles.

Once. Before the pregnancy,
it feels like a lifetime ago
a woman warned me.
She said, "Be cool, baby.
Watch out for those boys."

Disposables

My seventeen-year-old body
had barely turned eighteen,
still flushed in immaturity
a hot-headed teen who gave birth to a child
rigid behind a mouth puckered
in defeat at mom's refusal
to pay the cost of disposable diapers
for her jobless, no-income child.
"Paper diapers are too costly."
Her displeasure detected
in her tone. Mom pushing
the cloth diaper held between my fingers
down into the toilet bowl,
forcing the movement of soiled flannel
dunked in swirling motion.
My upper lip squeezed against my nose,
desperate to thwart the stench
that spiraled up. While I behave like
a two-year-old experiencing
icky fingers for the first time.
Not even looking down at what
my hands are doing.

Sullen at having to do
the dirty job of rinsing my own
baby's cloth diapers.
Unprepared for the truth
of what my body had produced.
Warped ideas of a newborn
impressions of a dolly of cuteness and fun.
Sniveling over mom's escalating
dissatisfaction as she continues to force
my hands to swish back and forth
until the fabric is poop-free
enough to wring out
and place into the dirty cloth bin
readied for pickup by the
baby diaper delivery serviceman.
Only to repeat the steps
all over again.
While momma blurts out,
in an earsplitting pitch,
"Grow up!"

Newborn Queen

A heart so precious,
my daughter, who when a child
if naughty, which was rare,
merely a whisper of
"I'm disappointed in you,"
would generate a torrent of tears
no belt, hairbrush, extension cord, or
willow tree branch needed.

A spirit so generous,
embracing with all she has to give.
Letting you know every time she sees you,
every spare moment she declares,
"I love you, Mommie."
Even today, as a grown woman.

Emotions so tender
that she'll cry through the night
after watching a sad movie,
or when she feels hurt.
Aching from sorrow, pain, or
betrayal in a film or real life.
Shedding tears at the shooting range,
the thought of ever having to
point a gun at someone, even

in self-defense, overwhelms her.
Those tears do not diminish her.
They represent her beauty.

A heart so grand, encircled
in spiritual strength that safeguards
and shields you in her love as she
wields her vigor through both
prayer and might.
She feels you.

She is my Onyx, my soul connection with the spirit
of her ancestors coursing through her veins.
She was my princess.
She is today a Queen.
She is loved.

For Precious Little Black Girls

Who dreams big and envisions hope
more vast/more immense than
the whole of the universe.
Who looks beyond the limited sight of others.
Laden with aspirations that scale mountains
and rise above clouds to crisscross
the immense ocean.
Pure, innocent, and easily hurt by the sting of pain
but refusing to give up.
Rejecting the surrender and ascending defeat
while rising through challenges
replaced by daydreams and optimism.
Who finds safe spaces below moonbeams
that filter through the windows
as she shelters beneath the protective cover
of bedsheets/where dreams
continue undisturbed.
Dream little black girl.
Dream.

My mother worked the graveyard shift, 10:00 pm to 6:00 am. I readied myself/watching her car turn the corner on San Pedro Street. I climbed out the window, scaling down the roof, balancing myself onto the brick wall separating the front yard from the back. The coast was clear.

The party was at Linda's house.

Par-tay

Hips rock from
side to side.
Motion infused by
throbbing music
over steam-filled rooms and
sweat-stained bodies of
wall-to-wall teens.
Roaming hands towards the
naughty places.
Ensnared by flirtatious
faces dancing to the
reverberating beats.
Jerking/Popping/Dropping
Tipsy from spiked drinks.

Intoxicated by the
Grinding/Humping/Bumping
Tongue-kissing
Funky vibes arouse the senses of
rhythmic girly curves
discovering sensual movement and
moments/sparked by
rapid soulful
rituals of sound
soaking the room

like sun-showers.
Moments when innocence
fades and disappears.
Before time to
hurry back home.

He Has No Clue

He has no clue what happens to the psyche of a woman/wife in her inmost heart during the evolution of the making of a brand-new human life. He has no clue; unable to trade places, he will never fully understand the experiences of a woman. Even in love, he is oblivious to the true feelings of a living soul growing within a womb, steeped in liquid passion—the humankind taking shape and form in the confinement of space inside her. A woman's body yields to the tiny being who spends nine months vacationing through its growth cycle as it advances towards the birth process. Her lifeblood is that which provides the vitality needed for the developing fetus to float carefree en route to an unknown future. The internal transformation that takes place as the essence of a child assembles.

A hand against a belly to feel life pressed against the interior of her stomach is no transfer of her personal experience to you. The fear, the joy, anticipation of the moment contractions begin and new life sails into the world through an area that expands in wondrous amazement—and the miracle can cross over to embrace a newfound reality.

He has no clue.

Jacalyn Eyvonne

Chapter 5

bat·tered

noun

1. "I had a dream I was being battered, but when I opened my eyes, I discovered it was real."

Jacalyn Eyvonne

Bill H. – Before Frank

I could taste the saltiness from the sea as the wind whipped against my skin and through my hair. A flock of seagulls glided above the waves as I strolled the sandy shore—mother ocean squishing between my toes. Suddenly, Bill's voice swept past me. His angry pounding in the background grew louder and louder as the clear sky quickly plummeted into darkness.

The loud knocking startled me from my sleep just after midnight—the urgency in the deep, stern voice called out.

"Police!"

I met Bill in 1972. I was twenty-one. Butterflies fluttered in my stomach when he approached me. The whirlwind relationship sucked away my breath, fast-tracking into us living together in the duplex he owned with his mother. We were upstairs; his mother lived in the downstairs unit.

Bill was a striking six foot five inches tall, a sharp dresser, and quite handsome in his rich-chocolate brown complexion. His brown eyes radiated behind eyeglasses that gave him an intellectual look.

He also didn't think twice about spending money on me. We ate at the finest restaurants and danced the night away at the most fly Los Angeles nightclubs. I felt like a queen.

Bill drove an all-white-on-white Fleetwood Cadillac. It was clean. The ride was so smooth it seemed to float down the highway. Whenever we traveled in that car, my daughter Nicole, three years old, would chime with delight, "Magic car, mommy, magic car."

Bill's second vehicle was a brown van, his business on wheels, selling counterfeit cassettes and women's clothing. Bill dressed me in the finest clothes from his collection.

Peddling bootlegged tapes was illegal, and the number of people selling unauthorized recordings at the swap meets surprised me. Bill walked away with weekend sales making an easy eight to nine hundred dollars a day, a large amount of money back then.

Word spread, whispering quickly across the swap meet whenever the Feds were on the grounds. Bill quickly gathered and packed the cassettes before the Feds got to him. A few were damaged from the rushed tossing into the back of the van.

I loved going to the swamp meets with Bill until the first time I realized that this was really something you could go to jail for, and I was scared. After seeing him rushing to pack up his merchandise before the FBI made it to his booth, I no longer wanted to tag along.

At night and during the week, Bill would station himself in various high-traffick shopping areas and nightclubs, selling out of his van. He used that time to schmooze the ladies to increase his clothing sales. I never accompanied him on those weekdays or evening club runs.

Months later, things changed. Bill beat me. They weren't just beatings; they were assaults, and he seemed to take great pleasure in them. I can't recall why or what sparked his violence. I only remember my fear.

The pain from the heavy belt strokes made me feel like I was leaving my body. Transported back to my childhood, reminded of when my mother would spank me using her belt. But his beatings were nothing like the spankings I received from my mother.

The belt wielded across my back made me crouch in a corner or scramble along the floor like a wounded animal trying to escape. No amount of my tears or screaming stopped Bill. He beat me until he was ready to stop, not because I couldn't take it anymore.

For a moment, I glanced at the moonlight drifting through the window. I thought about how I saw the beauty in the glowing light beams. Glimmering rays fell on the carpet while non-stop lashes whipped across my back and legs as I dragged myself toward the closet. After making it to the cluttered space, I inched beneath the clothing hanging over my head. Bill slammed the closet door shut and told me not to come out until he said so. Short of breath, wheezing, and gasping through tears, I rested my head on a pile of crumpled clothing in the corner. I lay motionless, obeying his orders. What he didn't know was that I welcomed that closet. It was my refuge, my sanctuary from the pain.

We went downstairs to his mother's house the following evening for dinner. She always cooked. It was a part of our daily routine.

The usual small talk ensued.

"How was your day, son?" she asked.

As he answered, their voices faded. I could see Bill's mother's mouth move but not hear her words. After the beatings, the overwhelming anxiety often transported my mind elsewhere. At that moment, I wondered what his mother was doing while I screamed over her head the night before.

Was she sleeping?

Was she cleaning?

Did she turn up her TV to drown out the sound?

She must have heard me. How could she not hear the screams and cries last night and the night before? Or the sound of my body thumping against the floor above her?

Is she that heartless?

She glanced in my direction with an ambiguous smile and asked if I wanted seconds. I shook my head no and looked at my plate. It was still full.

I was unaware of how I was going to save myself. Bill towered next to my five feet four inches. He was stronger than I was and didn't want to let me go. I was anxious about what was going to happen to me. How hard would I have to fight or how loud would I have to scream—to save myself?

A week later, the loud knocking on the door woke me from sleep. The pounding frightened me as it grew more intense. I approached as a voice yelled out.

"Police!"

The two police officers could see me through the glass panels on the front door, with one inquiring if I knew Bill. After opening the door, I responded, intimidated by their presence.

"Yes, he's my boyfriend."

That night, the officers informed me that Bill was dead. Shot in the stomach during a robbery. His body was recovered inside the back of the van. The clothing racks in the vehicle were empty, all the garments and money gone, the DVDs scattered on the ground.

The following day, family members raided our duplex. Faces of people I had never met shoved me aside and took everything of value. Wincing at the loud voice yelling "Bitch, get out of the way," by a man-relative of Bill's. I held my daughter tightly in my arms without resistance, bullied by their presence. All of this took place with his mother's blessing.

I had to report to the police department the next day. Once there, I learned that Bill's mother accused me of having him murdered. I couldn't believe it. I sensed she might have felt I was taking her son away from her, but I did not know she hated me that much. The police asked me to take a lie detector test, and I agreed.

The officer interviewing me said he understood Bill beat me.

"How did you feel about Bill striking you? Did you want revenge?"

I remember frowning in confusion at the question, finding myself gasping for air while holding back my tears. Wiping my cheeks as a few escaped my eyes and slipped down my face.

"Of course not! No! I didn't like him hitting me, but I don't know what happened to him."

I felt demoralized as my mind grappled with raging thoughts.

"That old lady had heard me screaming. Bill's mother knew what was happening above her head, yet she said nothing."

She told the police that she thought I had set him up, and it was easy for the police to assume it was true. That I had something to do with the crime.

Although I was in my early twenties, a fragile young mother, we're all criminals, no matter our age, if covered in black skin.

The following day, I moved back with my mother. I left everything behind except our clothing. The polygraph found no involvement or guilt on my part.

I never heard more from the police, Bill's mother, or news about the capture of the murderer.

I do believe that had Bill not died, I would have.

I Love You

Soothes the pain of
bruised flesh
painted across my body
when anger mounts
ahead of sorrow.
Stilling the uneasiness and
the onslaught of fear
shrouding me like
lightening striking
a hickory tree
burning my soul away slowly.
Compelling a barrage of
warm tears,
smothered and wiped
away by fingers
that caused the pain.

Makeup hides my reality.
Paints over the sadness and
moves me past each
eggshell-filled day of
waiting for tomorrow's storm
to come again and
wash away
the few moments of

contentment
until it happens again
and the calming words
I love you is repeated.

Last Night

When the beating stopped
he cried, apologetically
his tears rolling into mine
while crawling on top of
my wilted body.
Painful kisses against lips
oozing with blood from open wounds.
Assuring me it wouldn't happen again
like the night before, and
the night before that.
Stroking my hair over regrets
with fingers that only minutes before
rolled into pummeling fists,
now trying to seduce me back
from an unresponsive body
voicing subtle accusations entombed by
controlling, obsessive love.
"If you hadn't made me so mad."
"If you'd just stop talking back,"
only reassures me it
will happen again
blaming me for my beating.

What Are You Afraid Of?

The aggressive obsession crept
into the relationship.
Cloaked in devilish grins
and sensual kisses, before
a drink too many, an angry outrage.
Where a burnt steak or an unmade bed
provoked volatile warnings.
Before the slap, before the punch
Before the, I'm sorry flowers, and
realization of knowing
it's never a one-time occasion
after, the outrage surfaces.
The apologies and promises of
"It won't happen again."
The anger in your voice.

"What are you afraid of?"
He was stern in his ask,
beneath cold, repeating eyes.
And through raw tears and
shallow breaths, I whispered my reply.
"You."

In That Moment

Unlike anything you've known before
no experience can match
that feeling of ultimate betrayal
of the love you have given willingly,
the lust you've shared,
the warm touches
beneath silk sheets and
the smell of lavender on your pillows.
It is in that moment
abuse reveals itself
as insults and devaluing begin.
When confusion and disbelief
take hold and the doors of depression
open wide to engulf your entire being
In that moment
unimaginable truth exposed
all trust is loss
and panic enters the room.

I Am Concerned About You

The bleakness in your eyes
leads me to believe pain
exists within you.
Your playful heart
and bubbly spirit is absent.
Cheerfulness shrinks as
your vitality drifts
farther away.
Your dismay makes me weary,
I wonder where you have gone.
Where is the happy girl that grew up with me?
The playful one
who laughed aloud as the swing
whipped you high into the air
while sturdy legs pumped
pumped forward and backward.
Motions more forceful than
any of the children
swinging beside you, including me.

Your joyful spirit taking hold of
all of us, watching you gripping hard,
moving towards the clouds, the dreams,
the sensations of freedom,

as the wind glided
through your hair and
across your face. Floating,
filled with laughter that
spills throughout the spaces
surrounding all of you and
into all of those around you,
wanting to be like you.
How do I find her again?
I am concerned about you
fading away forever.

Beyond The Window

The world calls out to me.
Spellbound by the movement
of life, of shared love,
and dreams achieved.
Where I can leave behind
emotional scars and feelings
of despair.
Beyond the window
away from defeat,
the lashing out that injures
my happiness, to say goodbye
to the dying flames of my relationship
when living for others
means leaving myself behind.
Frustrated at being taken
advantage of,
I wish I were beyond the window
Looking in only for a moment
at a place where I am
no longer forced to be.

Authorization Not Granted

A chiseled face/unsmiling eyes
stare her up and down.
The tattered blouse bared her shoulder.
He scribbles on his notepad
in his blue uniform and shiny
badge/over the sound of tears
escaping like water sloping down a
melting glacier/along with it, she dissolves.
"So, to be clear, why did you go with him?"

An aching vagina/re-traumatized
on the exam table/the speculum still
inserted. Her body jerks/a reaction,
to the doctor's touch and
discomforting intimation.
"No need to cry; it's less painful than having sex."

The night scarred/an unseen barrier of
night-terrors as the sandman slumbers,
between her and her husband.
She can't yet do the thing that he loves.
Love back.
Emotions entwined with the
uneasiness in his eyes.
"Why can't you let it go?"

Words spurt from her mother's mouth
robotic in the repetition/the
"I told you so," judgment surging
in the background/no smart mouth rebuttal
just sadness/to run/escape
to the bathroom retreat.
There is safety in the room with the toilet.
"Didn't I tell you to stay at home?"

The open bible spread between his hands
forcing unquestioned acceptance.
Her pastor's fingers trace the words
as sonant imputations of guilt
slip from the folds of his lips.
"Galatians 5:19: Now the works of the flesh
are manifest, which are these;
adultery, fornication, uncleanness, lasciviousness,"
His offending voice continued,
"I've missed you in church."

Dead air of silence surrounds her
reticent thoughts/breathing in and out
the bible closed/books piled atop
in the room's corner.
Angry at God.
Angry at people.

She wonders
'How big hell must be,' hoping
it has room for others.
Disappointed by
uncaring words,
troubled by the lack of
understanding as
the shadow of her rapist
lingers with her at night.
Wondering why
people won't concede that
"No means No."

Real-Life Ain't No Fairy Tale

My fairy-tale
the one I craved
like ice cream on a
fiery hot day,
didn't end with me
being beaten.

Almost

I was almost that woman
caught up in crime because of a man
That woman that I often see and wonder
What the hell was she thinking?
Loving a man so hard
that she fails to love herself.
Fails to wrap herself in commonsense.
Knowing that what he is doing is wrong, yet
remaining in his unsafe path, wondering
what makes a woman so weak and needy
for his love, rather than loving herself, loving
him so that she chances crime, risk jail, believing
it will be alright; instead, winding up a resident
in a two-bed prison cell surrounded by strangers.
Critical of that woman's weakness, until looking
back at myself and realizing
I was almost that woman until he died.

Jacalyn Eyvonne

I Am Not An Inconsequential Word

Jacalyn Eyvonne

Chapter *6*

big·ot·ry

noun

1. "Her bigotry was the first time I ever felt a bee sting, my reaction to the severe hurt was allergic."

Jacalyn Eyvonne

Knock-Knock; You Can't Come In

I was exhausted from running but couldn't stop, finding myself fighting against a repeated cycle of closing doors. Up ahead, another door was slowly closing.

Faster, faster,
keep going,
don't give up,
I can't, I won't.
I will break the cycle.
There has to be an opening just ahead.

Doors have closed on me too many times to count, so many times that you would think I came with a springboard implanted on my backside.

Whenever I found myself pushed down, I got right back up. Some days, bouncing back might be slower than others, but it always happened. I have always recovered and found my way to move forward.

I am no superwoman, far from it. I believe, however, that when someone says you can't come in, I am more determined today to show that I can.

I wasn't always like this. When I was younger, closed doors hurt me. People hurt me. It takes time to mature and recognize that other people don't define who you are. And that is okay. When you're young, you get a pass. You're allowed to take the time to build confidence and resilience.

Embedded within me is the memory of when I went for a job interview. Gosh, I was desperate. I barely had the money for gas to make it to my appointment. The retail price of a gallon of gas around 1974 was 39 cents. But believe me, that was a substantial number when you had no money. I also had no food and a young daughter at home to feed. I was desperate.

I called on Father God with every footstep, walking up to the reception area. I was optimistic. If anyone knew how badly I needed the job, it was God, and he would not let me leave without securing it.

The lady interviewing me appeared professional in her sharp red suit. She was mature, attractive, and white. She had a big smile when she entered the reception area and called my name. The smile disappeared. Her entire demeanor changed when she saw me.

Behind the closed doors of her office, she became rude. She snapped at my every response to her questions, no matter how hard I tried to fit the mold. I dressed the part, wore my Sunday best, kept eye contact, and was on time for the interview. I sat up straight and smiled. I even used my best speaking voice, ensuring I avoided my natural at-home black vernacular. I code-switched, changing my diction, making sure I was talking white.

Then she asked, "Why would you think I would hire you?"

Her comment caught me off guard. It was then that I knew she was also racist. I responded.

"Well, I work hard, I'm dependable, and I can type fast."

She laughed in my face and said, "I don't hire black people."

I barely made it back to the car. My legs nearly collapsed under me. After climbing into the car, I sat crying. Shaking from disappointment because I needed that job. My life was in such shambles, and I didn't know what I would do. I'll never forget how hopeless I felt walking out of that office. It crushed me. I thought God had let me down.

I was an unmarried young woman with a child, living in a one-bedroom apartment on Normandie Avenue in Los Angeles, and I was black. I only wanted to feed my daughter and keep a roof over our heads. Waking up and getting through each day was hard. Privileged people don't realize how difficult it is for those struggling to survive.

Unbeknownst to me, it was a good thing. I would have given anything to walk out of there with the job. Later I realized that this racist woman did me a favor by not hiring me. She stopped me from further degradation and abuse, which I would undoubtedly have faced at that company. She shut the door on me and would not let me in that day.

After my 30-minutes of self-pity tears, I dried my eyes and drove home. I swore I would never let another racist white person bring me to tears like that again.

The next day, I started going through the classifieds as though the day before had never happened. I landed a job as an "0" operator with the local telephone company. God hadn't let me down after all. He wanted me to reach down into my heart for my strength and resolve.

Swing Hard Into The Night

Sing the blues of discrimination.
Bang out the phrases of
vivid stories of people.
Move to the sounds in that soulful,
no-nonsense groove, protesting the
challenges of history.
Listen to the bittersweet sound
of R&B, Rhythm and Blues,
post-bop jazz, as you fight on for justice.

Swing hard into the night,
moving to the irresistible rhythms
of legends.
Dizzy, Coltrane, Cootie, and Monk.
Move your body and mind
towards the fight for justice, as the
music of the cream of the crop
helps you sing, swing, and do your thing,
To Zoot, Hinton, Basie and Young, as
Ellington's code of perfection,
lodges deep into your soul.

Move those hips from side to side with
arms raised high in clenched fists.
Move hard, as the lyrics and music provide you

Strength to finish the fight for your rights.
Raise your voice as the delicate sounds of
R&J, Rhythm and Jazz,
progressive, cutting edge, mainstream
surrounds you in the background.

Swing hard to that soulful stuff
and the deep sad tunes of
Holiday, Ellis, Simone & James.
Wringing tears like Mann's flute.
And, in the deep of the night,
Gordon, Roach, Hancock, and Blakey
play on with cool dignity.

Raise your voice
Rouse your desire
Lift your spirit for your rights,
for your vote,
for your cry for freedom, and
the salvation of your soul.
For your life!
Fight!

Clinch those fists together,
Fighters, kneelers, prayers.
Swing harder.

Beyond My Skin Color

I am a woman
with the same
woman needs as you.
Because I am the
opposite of white,
doesn't mean
my black skin,
makes me the
opposite of you.

I Have Enthusiasm

I have intention
I have worth
I have boundless energy (sometimes).

My mind explodes with creativity,
Full of ideas and visions.
I dream of words and pictures,
both pretty and sometimes ugly
but my words manufacture complex
photorealistic images
I am my individual body of work and
what I offer is myself
through my ideas, my words,
my thoughts all on paper
or from behind the lens of my camera.
I am a writer, a producer, a photographer,
a director. I am me
being what I want to be.

Devoted

Lives ridiculed for too long
burdened by society's narrow-minded
belief of who you are.
Judged a nothing man.
Mocked and treated as
damaged goods.
A dumping ground for mislaid emotions and
uninterrupted hate, as though chains, still
bound your neck.

I kiss the spilling tears of pain
falling upon your face while you fight daily
between harshness and hope
repressing the mountains of human lips
that belittle and show disdain.

Over 400 years of strength impresses me
rising against the price you have paid, as
you blaze the winds of hostility.
Enduring nights filled with chilled echoes
from centuries of suffering.
Where each day begins with implanted feet,
on soil made fertile by the
blood of your likeness.

Living the horror stories of being born with
pigmented shades of warm
browns and cool beige.
Shadowed in death by eyes
too blind to know your gentleness, too
objectionable to feel your love.
Too uncaring to see the courage in
your resolve.

You are so deserving of a moment of
brooding, as you convey the hurt of the
endless moments of
blurred images of your life.
The chains are gone,
but the shackles of
bitterness remains to bind you.

My devotion is to you,
Black man.
For you have never been a
nothing man to me.

Ghosts of Past

Occupants of times gone by,
troublesome memories from long before
vengefully resurfaced, seething with
past behaviors that cause the
same dismay.
Now etched into our behaviors to
pressure our resolve.
Hatred forced to wander through ruins
that function to impede our lives.
Enveloping us in their wrath of
judgment and mounting lies.
The haunting weighs heavy
materialized from hiding places
as ghosts crawl out of slumber,
to emulate plethoric thoughts
sown deep within white ancestral trees.
Now hallowed beneath privileged skin,
passing on polluted thoughts
spirits goaded by crimes of history
meet us face to face once again.

Beginning

I wasn't born into slavery
but racism spit me
into existence
by attacking the color
of my skin.
I am the person I am
not because of you,
but despite you.

Hands Off

Don't touch my hair.
Hands off my locs.
My natural glory
my royal knots
Thou-shalt-not-touch
my cornrows/my kinks.

Step back from my afro,
my braids/plaits/my naps
Don't reach for my twists.
Stay away from my curls.
My faux is my faux
and my lace is
off-limits to you.

Your hands are out of bounds
stretched in my direction
when there has been
no invitation extended.
My wooliness is not a toy
or a dog to be
played with or petted
for your entertainment.

Hands to yourself,
Go away from my puffs.
The area around me
is my space to step into
your place to step out.
Leave my dignity/my glory
My power/my pride.
Leave my crown alone.

On My Knees

In opposition to the brutality,
an outcry in protest
to the curbside judge and jurors,
who take away your breath.

Draped in blue with
the badge of protection,
pinned against chests.
Hiding the hate that lives
rent-free in the minds
of those who so easily choose
to stand on your bodies,
drive their knees into your necks.
Shielded by the brotherhood,
the fraternity of the
Good-ole boys' club.

On my knees in opposition
in peaceful protest and prayer,
to bring attention to
the abuse hoping that
I can be of consequence
and do my part to help
save your lives.

My knees represent rising
to the occasion
against your hate
against your corruption
and for the despair of those
subject to your abuse
regardless of the backlash.

Karma

Steering through the cosmos of humankind
searching for those to hit back at,
making way to decide the time and space
where unexpected consequences linger
readied in wait for good or immoral behavior.
Where misdeeds and wrongdoings,
deliberate acts of cruelty and misfeasance,
reviewed based on free-will decisions.
Breaths of karmic divining go unnoticed
filtered between inhales and exhales,
forced out from lungs of the observed.

Truth has no chance of escape
from the universal "watcher's" response
to conduct that does not echo the life cycle
of decency and morality.
The passage of years between villainy
will not be dismissed or forgotten.
Proclaimed religious or spiritual beliefs
offer no shield. Fate decides for you.
Karma will decide the moment and place
of your punishment or reward.

I Am Not An Inconsequential Word

I Am Not An Inconsequential Word

Chapter 7

mar·ried

adjective

1. "My heart pounded like bare hands beating a djembe drum when I heard the words 'I now pronounce you man and wife.' I was married."

Jacalyn Eyvonne

Frank R.

It was a feeling of suffocation and rage. Clashing with an individual's mind transports you into a traumatizing battle affecting everything you are.

Faced with moral, psychological, and societal issues, winning against such a formidable adversary is difficult. Especially when you don't realize what you are fighting.

My husband passed away on May 2, 2001, my mother's birthday. Still, it seems like yesterday. We were together for 27 years.

I met Frank in late 1974. He was a brilliant man with dual PhDs. He had a photographic memory and was the most intelligent man I had ever met. I worked part-time at the telephone company while attending The Fashion Institute of Design & Merchandising.

We began dating. Soon after learning I was pregnant with our son, we were married on August 1, 1979. My ten-year-old daughter was all smiles by our side during the private ceremony at the Los Angeles City Clerk's office. I won't forget how happy I was that day.

During the early years of our marriage, I did not know that Frank carried a secret with him. Issues brought back from his service during the Korean War and time spent in Japan resulted in tremendous mental and personal anguish. As brilliant as Frank was, he had trouble making enough income to sustain a household. He was a consultant, but his self-employed business was insufficient without another job. We found ourselves in continuous catch-up mode, always behind on everything; rent, food, and utilities, often in the dark for non-payment of the electricity bill.

I eventually realized there were severe problems. Frank suffered from sleep deprivation, restlessness, and nightmares. He was also terrified.

His fear took time to reveal itself. Frank was well-founded intellectually, but something frightening lived inside of him. None knew how afraid he was except me. I was the only person who saw that part of him. He was skilled at hiding himself from others. And there were so many moments when Frank was loving, kind, and funny through all the heartache.

By the time our son was eight, things had gotten worse. Frank would repeatedly empty bank accounts, forge my name on checks, and lie. His lies became so regular that he would lie to protect earlier lies. He was extremely convincing. We argued a lot. The raised voices later turned into physical fights, except this time, I fought back. I would never allow myself to be beaten into submission ever again. When things became volatile, my mind rewound to Bill. I could hear myself screaming as I crawled towards the closet, desperate to escape. That would never be me again. I learned how to fight back. Sometimes, I even threw the first punch.

I never knew all the horrors Frank faced as a young man while serving our country. He did not talk about it, even though I frequently asked.

Things continued to worsen over the years. Frank's behavior grew more erratic and dysfunctional. Baffled, I did not know what was going on with him. I only knew that his behavior and the verbal arguments began to take a toll on me. We tiptoed around him because his moods would abruptly swing from anger to fear to tears. He often cowered in the bedroom when bill collectors knocked on the door—sending our son to the door when I was unavailable.

Finally, after meeting with a doctor at the VA hospital in Los Angeles, he checked himself into a 30-day observation program. He only stayed two weeks. I never felt the doctors gave him the attention or testing he so desperately needed. Frank was not a priority for the VA. None of our servicemen were, especially those who were black.

In early 1990, I left Frank. There was such deep hurt layered in my marriage. The stress was too much for me to continue to bear, and I ended up in a women's shelter in LA, later landing at my Aunt Lena's house. It took a month to find a job and eventually earn enough money to move. Because of the growing crime in Los Angeles and living alone with my two kids, we packed our belongings and traveled to Oakland. My son, now 10, and daughter, 20, were with me, and we began our new life in the bay area.

Frank would travel from LA to Oakland to visit, and it was late 1991 when he moved up north permanently. It was hard not to love Frank, and a new beginning might help. After all, we were still married, and thus, we decided to try it again.

I cared deeply for my husband. It was impossible to turn my back on him. He lived with the trauma arising from his service to his country. I continued to believe in him, hoping that things would get better. They never did.

Frank slowly slipped back into his old ways. His actions became even more erratic. Still, Frank established his consulting business in the bay area. He worked with business clients, developing relationships with local ministers and politicians. He even opened a shelter for women recovering from drug and alcohol abuse. His outer appearance to any onlookers was that of a brilliant man, receiving government contracts and court referrals to his shelter. But the illness shadowing him was dwelling inside our household. It was as though he lived with a split personality. It was truly unbelievable.

I recognized that whatever was going on with Frank was affecting his behavior. We wound up back at the VA Hospital seeking mental health services. It was to no avail. No one would listen.

After spilling my guts to a psychiatrist about all the issues in our home. And sharing my concerns about Frank's mental stability, the only thing the doctor asked was, "Why are you still with him?" In other words, just throw the black man away because he has no worth, not even after serving our country.

It wasn't until February 2001 that I finally understood what was happening with Frank. A few months before, in late 2000, his memory failed drastically. He couldn't think. He struggled with his thoughts and words.

A brain tumor, glioblastoma, discovered that February was advancing to a dangerous level. During his service, there may have been a link between ionizing radiation, polyvinyl chloride, and lead exposure.

Cancer had advanced to where he could not make any rational decision on his own. Frank needed immediate surgery, or he would undoubtedly die. His pastor, Pastor Williams, and I met with the medical staff to discuss the suggested operation. We agreed they should move forward, and with the pastor's blessings, I signed the paperwork for the procedure.

After the surgery, Frank remained hospitalized. He grew worse with each passing day. On May 2, 2001, Frank passed away.

I visited Frank earlier on the day of his death. His eyes scared me as he stared up at me. I found myself polarized by stages of crying just thinking about his eyes. For a time, I became isolated and acutely depressed.

However, I finally had the answer to his behavior over the past twenty-plus years. I believe the tumor had been there for years, pressing against a vital part of his brain, lying dormant, waiting to take hold of him.

Medical evidence has shown that the long-term effects of radiation from the fallout of the atomic bomb dropped on Nagasaki and Hiroshima affected people for years. The bomb advanced one of the worst brain cancers known to humankind. Glioblastoma. I also learned that it could take radiation-induced brain tumors years to form, sometimes 10-30 years.

While serving his country, Frank took part in three or more of the official campaigns in North Korea, assigned to the Seventh Fleet at Camp MacGill, Japan. Frank spent three years receiving a Korean Service 3 Star, which denotes his engagement in combat in ten campaigns in North Korea.

In 1949, Frank served on the *USS Waccamaw*, a ship the United States Navy noted as among the vessels infested with asbestos.

In May 1951, the communists pushed back to the 38th parallel. The battle line remained in that vicinity of radiation for the rest of the war.

Frank's service to this country was how he became exposed. One million South Korean civilians perished. About 800,000 communist soldiers died, and 200,000 North Korean civilians died. Between South Korea, the United

States, and participating UN nations, approximately 150,000 troops died.

I battled with the Veterans Administration, which continually rejected his service history and that the tumor resulted from his exposures. However, I didn't see it this way. After Frank's exposure vulnerabilities, he did not receive proper medical care and testing after serving his country. During his service, he received radiation and asbestos fiber exposures, the nexus to his brain cancer. We, his family, suffered because the medical system has constantly ignored and mismanaged the health care of black people.

The quality of care is poorer, with some doctors failing us due to hidden or unconscious biases. Sadly, the color of our skin can affect the type of diagnosis we receive. I know that firsthand.

In 2011, I ended up in the emergency room. I had severe pain in my upper right chest that radiated into my back. The emergency room did the standard heart monitoring tests and asked the usual questions. With my heart monitor showing no evidence of a heart attack, the doctor told me I would be fine and could go home.

There was no issue.

I insisted they look further. I begged the doctor to see what else he could do. Something was wrong. After my plea, the doctor said there was one additional test he could do. A venogram, where they run dye through your veins to look for abnormalities. After the test, the doctor walked into the room. He was ghost-like when he told me the venogram revealed a series of blood clots, one in my right leg and three in my lungs. I remained in the hospital for six days. Had I quietly gone home, I would have died.

Inequities exist. Our symptoms are easily dismissed, and we're sent home with aspirin even when we are, in fact, dealing with serious issues.

After my husband passed, I started falling while dreaming. My body flailed as it tumbled through the air. I never knew where I was falling from or what was below me. Yet the frightening rush towards the unknown beneath me overwhelmed me.

The dream became more frequent, abruptly waking me from my sleep repeatedly. That jolting feeling was unsettling. A combination of the past, years of stress, loneliness, and loss. You can't be with a person for nearly 30 years and not miss them.

One night, after the feeling of plummeting startled me awake, I lay in the dark. My breathing became labored.

I'd had enough.

I forced my mind to return to the dream. Soon I found myself deep in sleep, frantically tumbling. I was falling with swiftness and rapidity, unlike what I'd experienced before. I stretched my arms out, and I soared like a bird. As I glided through the clouds, I could feel the breeze. I had taken control of my dream. It was so calming, and I slid into a deep sleep for the rest of the night.

Since then, I have been able to go back into an unsettling dream and change its course. I have been in command of my dreams ever since.

It also helped to believe that Frank finally found his peace.

Fragments and Memories

The painting has darkened over time.
It has become old and worn.
Remembering the solitary spaces
of loneliness, and
comforting reassurances that
it is OK to grieve the loss
and mourn passings,
while yearning
for the fragments of
reminders of pleasant days
and hopefulness.
The reclaimed moments of joy
and times shared,
of faces filled with laughter.

Dreaming more than once
of the images in the painting
the faded ones,
that have darkened so over time.
The one that brings back memories
of laughter still heard,
and faces still seen
coming through the door,
all the sadness discarded,
only the sounds of the good times
that feels so very real.

Remembrances

They have gone away
So gone the beauty
From my withered rose.
I shall shed two tears,
One for each.

The Day I Knew

When I fell in love with you,
my body spoke.
Silent to you/loudly to me.
Aroused by the excitement
of being in your company.
Barely able to breathe
as my heart raced
and my legs buckled
at the knees.
Before the words of love,
Escaped either of our lips,
I knew,
You were the one.

Nuptials

Before God, we made promises to one another
on that joyful day, filled with hope and excitement,
as the aroma of love and rose petals spiced the air.
Indescribable bliss coiled us together in celebration
of our devotion to harmonizing promises.
Surrounded by symbolic pleasures,
a rainbow bouquet, and rings.
"Will you take this man/woman
for better/for worse
for richer/for poorer?"
Simple words spoken, sealing the promises
from our lips, over the nervous happiness,
enveloping our faces.
Hands cradled/dewy eyes locked together,
eager for a lifetime of commitment
and unconditional love.
"In sickness and health,
to love and cherish forever
till death do you part?"
The words before our lips touch,
binding us together.
"I do."

The Sound of You

Beside me
soft breath sounds
when you sleep.
Rhythmical/melodic/gentle
ebbs and flows
rising and falling
against the emanating
warmth from your body.
Welcomed by my skin,
you nestled beside me,
a security blanket
bringing harmony
to my life.
Comforted by my
happy ending.

Abstraction

A distant saxophone
sounds of music like laughter
jumps across my ears
cool winds of springtime
lavish my spirits
sweeping me into the mist,
of an illusion
engulfed in my dreaming.
I dare not awaken.

Whispers

of airy kisses encircled by
the silvery moon mist of midnight silence.
All reasoning blurred,
leaving me vulnerable and aroused as his eyes
crawl across my body, over hot kisses
and fingers moving and pressing,
spiraling along the paths and ridges
that shape who I am.
Days long gone, lost,
when I was young
and in love,
pantomiming my responses
to the impulses of his touch.

Whispers
remembering the sweet sounds
of unseen sensual caresses from
closed eyes. Caresses,
complete with breaths of flattery
and steamy words speaking to the
hidden corners of my body.
Finessing, my secret places
deliciously enamored,
immersed in nastiness.

Whispers of days gone, lost.
Virginity departing long ago
still waves goodbye in the distance
while I yearn for those quiet words to
visit me at the stroke of midnight.
To come whisper to me once again.

I'm Mad at You

When illness hides itself
behind your eyes
often unrecognizable
behind your anger.
I'm mad at you,
knowing it's not your fault.
You didn't invite sickness in
It found you.
You didn't welcome it into your heart.
It settled there.

My complexity reflects
back at me when I look at you,
coupled with the guilt that
visits me by day.
Causing me to pick at my pimples
chew at my nails.
The ailment of your body
the weakness of your disordered mind
Being careful of emotions that
maneuver your moods
leaving me under
unwanted stress, and wondering
Why me?
Why this?

Why so much work to live
each day with you?
Wanting what eats at you to go away
the sickness that forces
me to avoid your eyes.

Exhausted by my caregiver role
yearning to return to the past of
more the lover, the hot momma
The sexy wife that I used to be.
Not an attendant only to your needs
or a curator of your life.
I'm worn down by the slow
chipping away at my spirit.
The vanishing of me, of whom
I was supposed to be.
Dreams held back,
goals neglected, for a life that
dealt me this/dealt me you.
I'm mad at you,
knowing it's not your fault.
Missing you,
now that you're gone.

Lost Coins

Into the wishing well
my coin sweetened by a kiss
as desperate words for hopeful moments
mutter in hushed tones past my lips.
I follow its descent, splashing into
the melodic rhythm of
burbled ripples,
elated at the coins crossing,
into the wells mystic waters,
wondering,
"When will my wish come true?"

Another day, another coin kissed and tossed
more sugary whispers of yearning anticipation
of the granting of desires by the
Guardian of the well, optimistic that
the wish might come true.
Waiting through the summer's heat haze and
winter rainbows.
Daydreaming for a better tomorrow.

First Moments

In the darkness
between the twinkles
of a single candlelight
beside the noiseless crackle
of the fireplace
sinking deep within a
blanket of warmth
on a growling leopard rug
soaring from powerful hands
clinching
creeping
sliding
across my hungry
naked body
not having to fake
orgasm.

Jacalyn Eyvonne

I Am Not An Inconsequential Word

Jacalyn Eyvonne

Chapter *8*

neg·a·tive

adjective

1. "The negative vibes around the neighborhood gobbled the children up like a whale, everyone swarming in its belly, trying to stay alive. It was then that I knew I had to fight like hell to save my children."

Jacalyn Eyvonne

Where You Gonna Go?

The parent association's announcement of an urgent meeting on campus was sudden. A gun had been retrieved from a student's backpack earlier that day.

I have a decade between my offspring, ten years between my daughter and son, and ten years between my son and grandson. After my son was born, reality hit, and concerns about his safety were more present. My biggest worry with my daughter was keeping those mischievous schoolboys away from her. With my son, it was keeping him alive.

The hostility against black males was rising, and violence in our neighborhoods escalated at alarming rates. Our children caught in the line of fire were just added to the statistics. On top of these fears were growing concerns about gun violence and guns in schools. Today, nothing has changed.

Over the years, the media and the judicial system have painted black youth as scary adults. Our neighborhoods are labeled concentrated combat zones of crime and pollution, disregarding the lack of community resources, poverty, homelessness, and other disadvantages. So, once you give birth to a black male child, we no longer just watch what happens to others on TV; it also becomes our reality regardless of where we live.

You wonder how a twelve-year-old can be so pulse-pounding intimidating that a police officer can gun them down. A black child, I don't care how young, frightens some people. I don't care how precious our children are to us, how loving and compassionate, how gentle; their sheer presence makes those housing biases in their hearts nervous.

The desperation of people living in neglected, impoverished communities is easy to understand. Faced with hunger knocking at the door daily or living in the dark without electricity or heat. Desperation can drive people to make wrong decisions that can forever impact their futures.

When my son was in high school, the comments I heard while sitting and listening to him and his friends did not surprise me. They were straightforward with me, often surprising me with their honesty.

Ka-ching!

Brothas living in the ghetto,
poor all their life
watching white folks chillin' in a
40-million-dollar house.
TV screens show your oversized closets
bigger than my rented house.
More money spent in one day
than momma makes all her life.
And you wonder why a brotha
picks up a gun or sells drugs
for fast cash/quick money.
Push your forty-foot yacht in my face, then
act like you don't understand
when I wanna 'romp in the land of luxury' too.

*"Some kids will pack a gun or knife to protect themselves, so they
won't get hurt. Some kids are just scared cause they're bullied
every day." -BigT*

How You Gonna Tell Me To Go Back Africa?

White people prejudge me
before I walk through the door.
Hurrying across the street, walking
on the curb just cause I'm coming.
I ain't thinking about you, white man.
Telling me to go back to Africa
when I ain't never been to Africa!
Next thing you know, here come the police!

It's easy to see how violence comes packaged with living in the city. Not just police violence but the violence that happens because of concentrated poverty and community inequities.

All communities have individuals who commit violence in their neighborhoods. It is not some strange phenomenon that only happens in black communities. However, higher crime rates in our communities occur because local leadership does not address inequities.

Over the years, the violence has spilled out from the inner-city neighborhoods and into the suburbs. And calling the police even for mental health or non-criminal situations can be deadly.

That evening at the parent's association meeting, parents were outraged and alarmed at the situation. A student had a gun on campus. A sincere concern indeed. However, I heard the common generalizations about black youth. The language used to disparage this kid was the same old rhetoric.

"The kid is terrible."

"He's a troublemaker."

"He's from a dangerous neighborhood."

The air was thick with anger at this kid; however, no one asked why. What caused him to bring a gun to school? Who was he trying to hurt? Was he afraid of something, and if so, what was he afraid of? What caused the fear? The opportunity for insightful conversation flew out the door over the loud voices.

Mass school shootings continue, often committed by non-black individuals. Police continue to shoot unarmed blacks, and black-on-black violence continues to rise because of neglected communities.

It's not the people.

It's not the skin color.

It's the conditions of living.

I moved from Los Angeles to Oakland to Vallejo. I wanted to escape, get up out of LA, and protect myself and my kids. Mental peace of mind is what I sought.

I continue to worry about my son; now, I also have a grandson to worry about. Still, police violence and crime continue to follow us, leaving me to ask, "Where you gonna go?"

The Talk

I share the fear of other mothers.
That the natural pigment of your skin
creates irrational fears
In those lacking self-compassion and
the failure to see good in others.
Sometimes it's an intense dislike or jealousy.
Others appear afraid of you,
Not because you're scary,
but because they live with perceptions that
create unwarranted fears.
I'm saddened it's like this, though
not sorry that blessings cover you
enveloped by your abundance of melanin.
Keep your eyes peeled, knowing
every cop is not corrupt.
But anxiety over your safety is my onus.
Be careful.
There is no safety in your body.
The bulls-eye centers on your back.
You are ground zero for the attack.
Racism, Prejudice, Discrimination, Bias,
Bigotry, Injustice, Intolerance.
Your black does that to them.
Hands up in the air,

hands on the steering wheel.
Don't reach into your pockets.
Say, "Yes, sir," and follow instructions.
Don't argue or talk back.
We're still an enslaved population
and this is not our freedom.
It's more important that you come home.

I fear for your safety.
Do not walk too fast.
Never run down the street.
Pull down your hoodie
so they won't perceive you as a threat.
Keep the outrage off your face.
Don't sing too loud.
Keep your car stereo on low. Too much
happiness might appear suspicious.
Watch the stop signs and red lights.
Be mindful of speeds.
If stopped, remain calm, cool, and collected.
Never raise your voice.
Polite keeps you alive, even though being
upset isn't illegal.
A smile may help, but not a loud laugh
they may view it as mocking.

The fear for your safety is fatiguing.
Yet you must not hedge your bet
the danger remains ever-present.
I didn't realize things would be this way
when I smiled at your pushes
against my belly or the pain
endured at your birth. Still, please don't
reach for your cell phone or make
unnecessary movements. Be clear, state...
"I'm reaching for my wallet in my right pocket."
"May I open the glove compartment?"
I understand white people don't have to do this,
they believe themselves privileged and are not
blessed with the noble heritage
of Black Kings.

The concern for your safety lives with me. It will
never go away, nor will worries subside.
As long as skin color unnerves the frightened.
You must insulate these words deep
inside, readied to shield you from harm, knowing
they are no ironclad fix, so to protect you
I'll continue to pray.

A Mother's Nightmare

Today, God took possession of my child
leaving a shadow to engulf the
wails of a throbbing heart.
My spirit overwhelmed with grief
Weeping, as death
rejoices at the seizure
of my child's soul
over voices in the distance
sounds of empathic woes.
Just another gang banger.
Just another druggie.

My reality, scarred by real-life sadness
as tears crawl down my face.
The past is now drawn into the present.
Recollections and flashbacks,
a race between passion and hate.
My little boy, cheerful and unaffected,
strides into his maiden voyage of life.
That first day at school, he was so cute
in his brand-new tennis shoes.
Now over the stillness of his body,
he lay covered on the street,
as expressions of ugliness
scream out in the name caller's paradise.

Just another gang banger.
Just another druggie!

In high school
future seemed so bright.
Making plans for him
college seemed far out of sight
yet filled with hope
and a yen for life.
I'm suffocating in my guilt,
Challenging myself with questions
from a checklist of what-ifs.

What if I had lived in a better neighborhood?
What if I had kept the reins on him tighter?
What if my choices and decisions were better?
What if?
Overwhelmed, tormented, blaming myself
for bringing him into this
money-driven maze life's quest.

Today, my child has gone away,
Motionless, a zippered bag covered
what used to be my precious child's face.
A bullet walked away with his life,

Now death walks beside him
gleaming with delight,
As they cart him off past
An assortment of characters in the crowd.
While I scream aloud,
"He's in your hands now, Lord!"
Cause he's gone now. He is gone forever.
Still, sarcasm rears, taunting
Over empathetic woes
Just another gang banger!
Just another druggie!
Just another lost soul!

Grieving all the mothers who have lost a child.

Category Angry

Branded/bitter/resentful/enraged
because she demands respect
speaks truth/wears her passion and rage.
Flagged as bad-tempered/hostile,
aggressive and loud.
Faced with negative stereotypes and
angry black woman tropes.
Marginalized because of her unyielding
strength/her sassiness.
Her straightforwardness garners
disapprovals/for her show
of righteous indignation
against wrongdoings.

Designated the head-bobbing
brow-raised eye-roller,
hands-on-her-hip
picture of imperfection
full of judgmental criticism
interpreted black-female fury/of being
sharp tongue/and foul mouth.
Her body mocked/as too masculine.
Yet, her anger is NOT invalid or unnecessary.
Her concerns are not any different from others.

Her refusal to remain silent
is not to be mistaken for caricatures.
Her unyielding strength/the lack
of understanding the social barriers
faced/gives her the right to
speak loudly
when making her voice heard is required.

Her anger is justified.
Speaking out against inequality
is necessary.
She is not just angry.
She is an "Angry Queen."

Tanda Called Today

Lost girl
shrouded in a woman's body
too much ripeness before her
years of readiness.
Coupled with a man-child attitude,
one that hides her true self
beneath hurt and pain,
yesterday and years passed.
Behind prison gestures
and tough-guy stance
learned from neighborhood streets.

Will you wear a dress this day?
Her mother asks. She, denying
her womanhood, hating it so,
longing for love and tenderness,
that she can understand.
Not feeling she must hide
who she is and who she loves.
Tanda called today.
With that thug/rough
wanna be tougher mentality
she needed to survive
on the streets/with her gun
cocked and loaded.

She was dealing crack, making
her bucks, hiding painful
memories of street-war stories
below her fake laughs.

Like the time she stole a white man's
ten-dollar bill, how he chased after her
knife wielded in his hand, yelling
"Get back here, you little black bitch!"
How she ran and ran,
out of breath, hacking/coughing.
Her fourteen-year-old grown/schoolgirl
body/worn and beat/aged
from drugs/heavy from bosoms
too weighted for her slight frame.
Him right behind her.
"I don't know how that white man runs so fast,"
she'd say, winded/laughing/knowing
her laughter was not genuine.
Nonstop running until she couldn't run no more.
Until he caught her, and she had to give
the ten dollars back.

Tanda called today.
Back out on the streets
packing her loaded gun
still dealing her crack.
This is your last lap,
no longer the little girl,
only got one strike left to go!

Will you pray with us?
Lord, bless this child and keep
her safe as you
keep others safe from her.

*A Short Story based on the poem "Tanda" appears in the book
"Strange Things Happen at Midnight" titled "Apgar House."*

Without Words

Imbued to hear beyond
unsaid words
and silent struggles.
Beyond the laughs
Beyond the cries.
Hidden behind fresh-faced
innocence and distant eyes.
The troubles that live in unsettled
movements of raised brows
and unhappy lips.
Distractions that hide anxieties.
Beneath the sorrow.
Beneath the pain.
The crowning challenges
of motherhood/Listening
to what has been unsaid.

The Keeper of Souls, The Bearer of Pain

Beneath the moonlight and the sounds of dry thunder,
The Keeper of Souls carries the pain of thousands.
His body stands cloaked in the virtue of the hearts
of the masses, whose stories course through his veins,
and the lines of our lineage weave through his flesh.
Assuring that those who suffered the brutality of life,
oppression of enslavement, separation, and death,
are never forgotten, but live on within him,
as histories remembered.

He, entrusted with the power to breathe existence
into the legendry of their misery, honors the will of
our forefathers, passing ancestral strength through
conscious knowledge and wisdom to the rest of us.
He is the black man, imbued with the seeds of history.
He is the custodian of bodies.
The Keeper of Souls, the Bearer of Pain, and Guardian
to the Lost. His skin chaffed by the
heartbreak of thousands.
Grounded in the narratives of fallen generations.
He who appears beneath the moonlight
amid the sound of dry thunder. Our reminder
To celebrate the spirit of our ancestors.

A reminder to all black boys growing into black men.

I Am Not An Inconsequential Word

Chapter 9

ma·tri·arch

noun

1. "The shoes were loose when I stepped into them, becoming the matriarch, fierce like a giraffe poised to decapitate a lion with one kick to protect my family."

Jacalyn Eyvonne

Behind The Brown Eyes

I'd just poured my morning cup of coffee when my son Neuman rushed into the kitchen with the news.

"Mom, Kevin got arrested."

Kevin was Neuman's best friend. They were inseparable. His striking brown eyes, set beneath lengthy lashes, drew me to him. Each time I looked into them, I wished they were mine. I mused, telling my friends that I had given birth to twins even though they looked nothing alike.

It was late 1991 when I asked Grammy, Kevin's grandmother, to let Kevin come live with us for a while. Los Angeles had frightened me, even though I had lived there much of my life. But, by late March 1991, the entire city felt different. Every news media network covered the Rodney King beating on March 3rd. You couldn't escape the images of the violent blows to his body. The city of Los Angeles felt as though it was spiraling downhill.

Gang violence in Los Angeles continued to be a growing concern. I worried about my son's safety each time he stepped out the front door. Taking the color of his clothing into account was another consideration.

I spoke to Grammy about Kevin's shirts, suggesting she avoid sending him out in red or blue. The colors stood for the two dominant street gangs. Each was vying for power, holding South Central Los Angeles and the city of Compton hostage within their grips.

I recall driving through Compton. On a hot summer's

day, I wore a bright red blouse. I realized where I was, in the Compton Crips territory. I threw a sweater on top of my blouse to cover the red. It was 90 degrees that day, and my car had no air conditioning.

South Los Angeles had been our home, and gang territory was becoming difficult to avoid. Each time I looked at Kevin and Neuman, I knew they were becoming ripe, prime targets for recruitment. The thought of them wandering into the wrong neighborhood, wearing the wrong color or a coveted pair of tennis shoes terrified me. I knew one misstep, one mistake, could get them killed.

Kevin's grandmother was raising him alone. Kevin's mother died from asthma exacerbation, intensified by illegal drug use. His father was in prison. Grammy was doing her best, but she was nearing 68, in poor health from stress, getting around on knees pained from arthritis.

Grammy loved Kevin, yet raising a young black male on the south side of Los Angeles by herself was difficult.

When I moved north to Oakland, I appealed to Grammy to let Kevin come live with us. There were gangs in Oakland back in 1991, but they were much less noisy than those in Los Angeles.

Bad things were brewing in Los Angeles. The feeling lingered deep inside me. A sensation that wouldn't go away. I would continue dropping hints about Kevin coming to live with us, but she was firm. I knew not to press her any further.

In Oakland, Neuman stayed in touch with Kevin. We were excited when she agreed to let Kevin come visit through the summer. It was great having him with us. The boys had the chance to get familiar with the new city and make new friends.

I'd hoped Grammy would change her mind and let

Kevin stay at summer's end, but she didn't. She insisted Kevin return home to Los Angeles. Grammy was getting old, and she needed Kevin's help. I understood her needs, so we all piled in the car and took the six-to-seven-hour road trip back to Los Angeles.

Grammy's face lit up when she saw Kevin, but it was a sad parting. Neuman was leaving behind his best friend again, and I left behind my other son. The drive home seemed long, but I was glad to be leaving Los Angeles. The city still left me with an unpleasant taste. Gang activity between the Bloods and the Crips dominated the news, and I sensed something was brewing beneath the surface.

Kevin never came back for another summer visit. Still, he and Neuman remained in touch.

Sometimes your coffee is a little off-balance; other days, it is amazingly flavorful. That morning, my morning cup was perfect. The aroma lingered past my nose when Neuman burst into the room with the news. I couldn't believe what I was hearing.

"Murder! Kevin arrested for murder!"

I immediately called Grammy. It was true.

Kevin was involved in a robbery gone wrong and arrested with gang members, who car-jacked a man and murdered him. Kevin would stand trial in court as an adult.

"If only Grammy had let Kevin come stay with us, he would be here, safe."

The broken and diminished sound of Grammy's voice saddened me. It was as though her heart were failing through the telephone receiver. Yet I knew I could not blame her. She did the best she could.

Gang activity took a turn for the worse in Oakland. We have since moved away and today live in Vallejo, yet the violence seems to follow. I am unsure where we can shield ourselves from the brutality that clouds many communities.

My son is much older today. I am thankful he has insulated himself from the violence that seems to engage and self-destruct the innocence of so many young people.

Kevin is now a tenant of the California penitentiary system, serving a 50-year sentence.

I will never know what happened to Kevin, why, or how. I can only speculate. Thinking about what would motivate him to kill a man only leaves me with questions without answers. He was an impressionable young man with eyes that would ignite a room. A mark in a jungle of divisiveness, raised by a woman too tired and old to keep watch and control.

I recognize that what is happening within our communities and youth is daunting. Their anger is released into a world fed by the hatred of their melanin skin. As violence rises, morality declines, and taking life seems routine and effortless among youth who sometimes kill without a thought—exposing anger at the world that feeds their rage with hatred.

We soak up the news, shrug shoulders at unruly behavior, and gloss through images of death and destruction pictured on our TV screens. As stolen lives continue to blanket communities, violence spreads among our youth.

I continue to sip my morning coffee. It has become my daily routine while skimming the internet or watching the news on TV. My observations of what is happening among our youth heightened after my son's birth. We need to find solutions. This morning, the headlines reported another drive-by shooting, another murder. The suspect a 22-year-old.

It is complex, living daily between contrasting emotions; I light up knowing my son is safe with me still today. Yet, there is sorrow about Kevin and young men who find their lives altered, some sadly meeting death.

I try to cling to the memory of big brown eyes and lengthy eyelashes. Eyelashes that I still wish I had, and the memory of a little boy, full of life, vigor, and energy rather than sorrow. Since then, Neuman became a magnet for friends, and I became the neighborhood mom. My home was the place where my son's friends would hang out. Many stayed over for days at a time because their parents didn't care where they were. These young man-teens welcomed the hot meals and soda pop, and it did not matter the number of mouths I had to feed.

Being a mom is hard. Being called mom by some of the roughest kids in the neighborhood is an honor.

Published in the 2013 collaborative poetry collection "Sistah's With Ink VOICES." This is the revised and updated version of "Brown Eyes."

War

When streets filled with muted smiles,
of strangers/speaking the language of strangers,
as Afro/Anglo worlds collide
because people give others hard times, as
neighborhoods grow increasingly surrounded,
by discarded emotions/cluttered
in a carnival-like atmosphere
of homeboys and rowdies/lovers/brothers/
and fathers loitering
outside of liquor stores
Mothers/rearing children in
fatherless households targeted
by the slings/arrows of poverty.
When lace-front wearing, long-haired,
short-skirted/bare-butt girls take aim with
flirty smiles during virtual encounters, and
young things stolen or coerced away,
trafficked, forced to turn to their uterus
while a laid-back pimp daddy or
commercial trafficker keeps a bird-eye view
on the investments.
It's Wartime!

The sweet innocence of youth/replaced by the perils
of death/Trap houses invading neighborhoods.
battle zones/day or night/shoot-outs
with opposing gangs/dealers, while
little five-and-a-half-year-olds
shot down in cold blood/playing in
their front yard/sleeping in a bed/riding in
the backseat of the family car/as an arm
hangs out the oncoming car window, a firearm in
hand/driving/firing/random/uncaring where
the bullets land/who the bullets hit/or how young.
Around the corner/a teen walks along the
avenue eating potato chips with his girl
until a car passing goes BOOM!
First thought a backfire/another teen falls dead.
It's Wartime

Smells of red beans and rice/pork ribs on the grill/linger
in the background, past boarded-up buildings with
broken windows and teenagers-rapping-in-synch.
Tent cities filled with the homeless/hopeless
All this, just another ordinary day
cause leadership/and police/ignore the iniquities
or make them worse.

Injustices overlooked for fear of reprisal; if you
speak out, you're threatened/a target/a snitch.
Forget your human obligations to one another,
silence rewarded/disloyalty dishonored.
Adherence to the rules of the street.

It's Wartime!
Time for decent folk to wake up/get-cracking/
stop pacing the floorboards/like overwound,
wind-up toys/turning your head to all that is
happening around you.
Time to take your neighborhoods back!

The Awakening

To unleash
The anger of the world
Upon the diminishing
Souls of men.
Impregnating their minds
With the frustrations
Of a suffering people.
With the eyesore
Of poverty
And the pulsation
Of pain,
Torturing them into
A conscious awakening.

Loving You

When you were little,
blowing kisses into ears
that stood from your face like
wings, made you giggle
as deep dimples stretched
across your cheeks resembling
large craters on the moon.
My little man.

I remember the last time you
sat on my lap and smiled up at me
before pulling away, akin to
a grown-up man full of pride.

"I'm a big boy now, mama!"
You bubbled. No longer needing my lap.
Climbing into the seat beside me in the
darkened movie theater. Your tiny frame,
unable to peek above the chair ahead of you.
Far too stubborn to return to the thighs,
yearning to be there for you.

That time you tried to hide your smile
when your first tooth came out.
I felt your embarrassment when the kids
laughed at you and called you snaggle-tooth.
The glow on your face when the
big smooth coin appeared
beneath your pillow.
You couldn't wait to get through breakfast
eager to show off the coin jiggling in your pocket
ready to take charge over the mocking
from the teasers the day before.

Those days of clutching your fragile little body
against my lap, or wiping tears to ease your
troubles until your sadness faded.

Through the years, the road to loving you
has grown, as you draw away from
me more each sunrise-to-sunset.
Fearless in your new manhood.
Torn between the 'boy-man' emotions
that come and go, like people in our lives.
I mask my hurt as you distance yourself
each passing moment.

Come back, my son
To the lap that shields you
From the hurt and pain.
To the heart that aches with you
through your despair.
To truth never hidden
a truth, which has always been.
To my love for you,
Forever. Still, knowing that I must
release you so that you can grow.

A Point of Fact

The seed of
my daughter,
my grandson,
this day a man.
Skin deep-rooted
in blackness.
Me, fixed
in my fear.
No foreseeable
end in sight
to the decay
and misery
of racial blight.

Run Little Black Child

Your mind says run!
But you can't.
There's a bullet aimed at your back.

Run because you're afraid.
But you can't.
It's used to justify your guilt

Run because you want to live.
But you can't
You're already dead.

Run until you are free.
But you can't.
Because you never will be.

I Am Not An Inconsequential Word

Jacalyn Eyvonne

Chapter *10*

day·dream·er

noun

1. "I was called a daydreamer early on and took flight toward the castle in the sky, musing in my own reverie, searching for my imagination."

Jacalyn Eyvonne

Reflections and Rituals

Magic lures me back into time, turning me into a giggling child, musing over a card trick or levitation toward the sky. Not the three cups and a ball shell game that happened on a city street when a fast-hand severed my sister from her twenty-dollar bill. But instead, the fun, mesmerizing illusions that entrance with sheer wonderment.

December is a magical month for me. It falls only days behind Thanksgiving when I spend time with family. We overeat and drink too much. We stuff ourselves for days and look forward to doing it again come Christmas Day.

It's the month I reflect on my past, my accomplishments or lack thereof, and outline my plans and commitments for the new year. I look forward to the festivities, the Christmas lights, the celebration and observation of Hanukkah, Kwanzaa, church services, food drives, reminders of Christ, or celebrating life and family. I find people more pleasant at this time of the year. More joyous.

However, my favorite part is revisiting that special Christmas Eve when I was a kid. The night I saw Santa's sleigh pulled by reindeer swooping past the moon—always wanting to remind my family that life always includes a bit of magic.

New Year's resolutions are an annual ritual for me. I commit to dieting, exercising, avoiding procrastination, and accomplishing new goals. Many times, I've found myself off-track. I've gone seasons without losing more than a few pounds and gaining them right back. Still, I try to create standards for myself each moment because I am determined to grow and evolve.

A midnight kiss, a toast to future prosperity, or the idea of cleansing past mistakes is my way of reforming myself. A euphoria comes with opening my eyes and realizing that I woke up in a new tomorrow.

Believing in myself is much easier now. Sometimes I just sit with myself and dream. I spring out of bed at other times, inspired by what just happened in my mind. Negative words don't hurt like they used to; they fall away like leaves preparing for autumn, moving out the way, so I have even more space to dream.

December 2016 was the first holiday season I would not hear my mother's voice. Her passing made me feel like I was strapped on an emotional roller coaster. My hair is much thinner now from the stress of losing her.

I don't care how strong you believe you have become; there are those challenging times when you must work hard to keep from falling back into traps that suck the life out of you.

I focused on all the beautiful things my mother did and said. The wonderful person she was outside of my nitpicking. I recalled our conversations and laughter. She loved her garden, so I bought myself bouquets of flowers to remind me of her. I smiled over old photos.

I last visited mom when she was in the hospital in Los Angeles. My daughter and I traveled from Oakland to Los Angeles to be with her. She was unresponsive. To this day, I don't know if she realized we were there. I'd like to think so.

I hope the sound she made as I whispered, "I love you," in her ear was her way of saying to me, "I know you are here." Clinging to that possibility makes me smile even more.

I regret not spending more time with her or saying I love you more often. The distance between us should not have been an excuse and left me wanting to hear her voice and hug her one more time.

The sadness of her loss often visits me, but I draw back into memories and know that she lives within me.

She is in the circling flight of birds, the falling droplets of gentle rain. When I want to dream of seeing her at night, I glance at the soft stars twinkling above.

My mother, Mattie West - Became a Diamond on May 4, 2016. I love you.

Dewdrop

A drop
of dew
wept
upon
the befallen
flower
as it
gracefully
faded
into
darkness.

Take Flight

Spread your wings
like the eagle gliding high overhead.
Across the world,
hovering over the dominion of hope.
Make your goals your reality,
wings slicing the air, lifting/thrusting
you forward towards your dreams.
Lunge sky-high above all odds,
plunging over the cloudy overcast of negativity.
Swoop, reaching out and grabbing hold
of expectations.
Keep going, go faster and faster.
Create your blueprint of purpose.
Stick with it!
Don't give up. Don't look behind you,
only look forward.
The journey is your adventure,
willpower is your reward.
Live/dream/cherish every moment of your flight.
Follow the eagle's wing wisps
leaving behind puffs of clouds
as you create the path
to all your desires.

The Woman

Hints of softness emerge
in a quiet aura of
lingering cologne smells
from the woman whose
unspoken promises spill
from the smile on her lips,
finally, in control of herself.
The woman.
Innovative, adventurous, strong,
who plays the game of winning and losing,
loving and letting go, getting
better at her liberation, better at the
man/woman stuff.
The woman.
She is ready now.

Older & Wiser

I once was the girl who hid in quiet fear
submerged/beneath disrespect and pain.
Wrapped in the arms of the popular guy,
sought after by all the girls.
Who looked so good/and flashed his money.
The one who drove a nice car/while I closed my
eyes to the dark, not knowing about the mistreatment
to come/from the bad boy with the fancy toys.

I became the woman that later
shouted/who roared back, determined
never to be bullied again,
refusing to take a hit without hitting back.
Me, both witty and angry,
sharp-tongued and readied for the boxing match.

I am now a woman, both older and wiser
who is at ease by the kindness of a man.
The soft words/gentle kisses/simple smiles
from sharing a touch/the company
we both welcome/mistakes from
our expired past left behind.

Today, I know the things I must do/accepting
the outcome of my troubled existence.

Empowered by me/in my aloneness
untroubled/as I look forward to more chapters
of my future/where sharing the world/
with myself is the reality of my present life.

Ready To Serve

My bitterness melted
softening like butter
sizzling
over a low flame
as I slowly
warmed up
to me.

Nicely Wrapped

Faded-blue jeans hug
the curvatures of her body
flows over thick hips and thighs
of curvy plus-sized ample regions.
Denim rolling across her
in perfect symmetry,
highlight the God-given molding,
a silhouette of etched sensual
angles hugged like an expensive,
iridescent black pearl preserved in a
Tahitian oyster shell.
Her wrapped frame
spotlights her shapely profile,
the epitome of femininity.
Keep your hourglass, apple,
and pear descriptions,
there is nothing unusual about her
blessings, not a thing unnatural
about the well-formed, sexy,
voluptuous she.

Skip Forward

Searching for that uncomplicated love,
that comes with little effort.
The fairytale kind of passion
that you grow up reading in storybooks
or see on TV shows.
Yearning/imagining the titillated
time spent behind locked doors
and closed windows.
Envisioning the ideal man/woman
sharing texted promises and
written kisses/across computers
and phones.
Hopeful words of promise typed out
in-where-you-can-pretend
to be spaces.
Desperate for a loved laced tomorrow.

Hope-sites, with gussied-up pictures
where cupid made commitments await
with paid membership fees.
Where lovelorn guys and gals hopelessly
ripe for the picking like cherries,
both sweet and sour, seek
utopian soulmates lined up in rows
of enticing stories and impressive pasts.
Meet your future.

Meet your match.
Meet the man/woman desperate for you.
Like you're desperate for them.
Sexy/Young/Handsome/Girl/Guy.
Cell phone pictures primed for picking.
Overflowing with fake promises and lies.
Eager for the imaginary touches,
the sweet assurances.

Prettier than anyone you ever thought
would be interested in you.
Welcome to reality and the sometimes
feelings/that bring you to your knees.
Being catfished/before realizing that
soulmates don't come easy.
It often takes more than a click on a
profile picture or pretty face.
God will deliver them to your front door
assign them to you when he's ready.
When they must ring the doorbell
of truth to get in.

(A kiss tossed to my daughter, who made a joke that inspired my words here).

Are you the one?

I want to jump
all the way
into love.
To find that person
that makes me laugh
and cry
with happiness,
to look at you
through hazy,
drunk with
passion-filled eyes.
Falling, rapidly
into your arms.
Captivated by you
romancing me,
me romancing you.

Are you the one?
To stir
My sexual fireworks
of rustling flames
high into the sky,
sparking trails of
pixie dust leading
to enchantments
that float me away.

Are you the one?
Where we fall
into an intense
fervor
and I breathe
you in over
and over
each day.

Un-Ladylike

She wanted physical love.
To be desired was attractive to her.
Less a fault, more
quality of her independence.
She drank a lot and smoked weed, and
when the popular boy took her
into the closet at a party. She obliged.
The sex in the closet felt good
until the door swung open.
The screaming girl outside said,
'he' was her boyfriend.
She called the girl whose skirt was up
A bitch and hoe. Though, refusing to
call her boyfriend, whose
pants/down below his knees,
any name at all, though
a part of the twosome.
Unbothered by the name-caller at that
moment, she straightened her skirt and
accepted her new label.

She felt like a woman who believed
orgasmic pleasures didn't belong
only to the boys.

A feminist before feminism,
before her time, a nonconformist
unruled by oppressive cult norms
of what a girl/woman was
supposed to be. She believed
in her right to act like any boy/man.
She wore her title well.
As the bitch.
Welcoming being the hoe.

A woman that didn't care because she
enjoyed the sex that felt so good,
outside and inside of her body
that she screwed everybody
inside and outside the closet
whenever she wanted to.
She didn't give a damn after that.

I Am Not An Inconsequential Word

Jacalyn Eyvonne

Chapter *11*

ste·reo·typ·i·cal

adjective

1. "Her stereotypical impressions made me want to beat her ass to show her she was right, but I didn't because she was wrong."

Jacalyn Eyvonne

Black Sheep

When you grow up with negative conditioning, somewhere in the back of your mind, it will affect you, especially if there is no counterbalance happening at the same time.

During my growth journey, I searched for myself around every corner. I struggled against society's brainwashing, the stereotypical beauty standards, not being light enough, and hair not being straight enough. Skin too dark, lips too thick, booty too big. I was fighting for self-purpose, emotional salvation, and struggling for acceptance in a world of unacceptance.

In contrast, I am jubilant watching black women thrive in their blackness over the past few decades, and I love it. Showing off who they are with pridefulness and not caring about what anyone thinks. Wearing their big puffy hair, cornrows, and braids, daring somebody to say something with their eyes. We reign on social media, on TV, and in magazines. There is an immense pride within those of us loving our God-given features, entering the realm of "Queendom-hood." I strut with overflowing self-esteem and self-worth. No one can tell me that my crown is undeserved.

In grade school, my classmates teased me, labeling me flat-chested, flat-nosed, and chin for my long narrow face. I wanted my nose to be shapelier. I wished my boobs were bigger, but I grew to love myself as years passed.

Back then, parts of me lived outside the norms of others' expectations. However, I was conflicted in terms of my personal growth. I had a long way to go, but I was fortunate to find the fortitude to save myself.

Sometimes, you become keenly aware of your self-worth before anyone, including your family.

I was always made to feel like an outcast, different. My thoughts filled me with dreams and goals others sought to lead me to presume were out of reach.

Dream Big

She was a dreamer, and she dreamt big.
Not wanting just a job, sensing
her boss woman qualities
Knowing what she could be
even if others didn't.
Owning her own company was part
of her dream. Making her voice known
in her own way. Discovering
who she was/is/will be/today.
She found her way.
She made it happen.

Unlike today, we had access to various extra-curricular courses like cooking, sewing, pottery, and even automotive. I became a skilled typist. My teacher encouraged my typing, not because she judged me proficient or fast, but because she considered that was all I could do. She explained that I needed to learn to type because I was best suited for a secretary or clerk role. My assigned counselor suggested the same thing. Neither tried to encourage me to imagine big or outside the box. My family was doing the same to me. My mother always told me to keep my clerical job rather than pursue my desire to become an artist or photographer.

While neither my typing teacher nor counselor said the words, I knew what they meant. My skin color was the restraint blocking them from seeing the actual me. Mom only wanted me to have a steady income, not seeing other possibilities.

As I moved forward, I also learned from them to keep my ambitions to myself. Their words plucked away at me, sucking my confidence away. It took some years to get back on track; however, I found my way.

I continued my photography, adding filmmaking to my skill set. Later, getting involved in real estate and becoming a broker in 1993. I sold real estate for over fifteen years, setting up a brokerage with 36 agents under my license. The brokerage was quite successful, netting me a sizable yearly income before the market crash in 2007.

Years ago, I landed at a place where I no longer let anyone tell me I can't, and I don't let the past define my future. People would never know what I went through had I not shared fragments of me because of who they observe before them today.

I was not born strong. Just as an infant will fall on its backside when learning to walk, I fell on mine. It took practice to become me and gain the skills to drive unhealthy habits from my life.

I talked about my springboard; I just had to learn to use it and not allow other people's words to define who I am.
I laugh out loud at the reflection of the world looking back at me, where big butts are now fashionable, and lips are being injected to look like mine. The irony of it all is quite comical as hate still looms.

Hate can still take a toll on you when it is clearly in your face, suppressing your votes and erasing your past. It can be depressing, but I've learned to take time to experience disappointments over the years, but not for too long.

I used to love to do this with ice cream. Today, I'm on an infinite diet, so the ice cream is only for fleeting moments. I may seek to talk to family if I need to and ask for help. I'll even research to determine how others are handling these moments. My dog is my hug. There is immense pleasure in funny videos or good movies. No matter what, I get up, never give up, and keep it moving forward.

An Erasure

The wildfire of polarizing ideas becomes
unfolding battles clashing, raising
dust on the battlegrounds of America.
Two parties readied and postured to fight.
One against the diversionary tactics
of perpetual ignorance.
The other, the one-sided red state
seekers fighting to WHITEN American culture
by forcing conservatism throughout the land.
Ignorance pushers and out-of-control white
'wokeness' declares the black experience
unimportant, an obstacle to the
minds of children.

Their lusty censorship spreading, bringing
archaic efforts to erase our existence from
history books. To whitewash
elements of slavery from classrooms.
Foolish cries against non-existing
critical race theories in our schools,
born out of callow ignorance.
Political evil, reckless desperation
prompt the return to the past.
A return to white superiority and privilege.
Back towards the days of servitude and
"Yes sir," and "Yes, ma'am."

Hiding your black experience while
re-experiencing former subjugation
in the present through the limiting of your rights
By attacking all that you are,
an excuse to avoid corrupting already corrupt
minds from the facts.

Banning books=banning Blacks.
Harmful to minors=harmful to white people.
Beloved is no longer loved
even The Holocaust is caustic.
Two parties readied, postured to fight,
One to erase, the other to stop the erasure.
We will meet on the battlegrounds of America.
Ready the truth infantry to the frontline.
Prepared for the ongoing attacks.

What do you see in the mirror?

The mirror peers back at
the panoramic view of umpteen grays &
sagging breasts & eyes pitted
shadowed from endless undertakings
to recapture bygone years.
Wailing like sounds of crying trumpets
as superficial efforts line up behind
crowded emotions/exhausted from
countless toe-touches/lavished fragments of
vanity & failed attempts to erase wrinkles.

The cracks lurk beneath heavily
coated complexions of powder
& paint & sculptured red lips,
keeping secret, the deep and present
fear of aging, of weariness
hanging on to lost seasons.
When your heart feels young,
but others reject you because of your years
as though becoming old is disenchanting
rather than a blessing.
Reinforced stereotypes that
you no longer are worthy of
self-worth.

The mirror waits for you to decide what
you want to see because age is relative,
your rite of passage is knowledge,
waiting to be shared with the world.

Glance at yourself with a new sense of
purpose as the mirror returns your stare.
It awaits your courage
to fight the negative perceptions
to realize the profound beauty that exists
within and radiates from
the splendor of wisdom held inside.
You have a voice in deciding
which reflection will be returned to you.
.

Rudeness

I ran into rudeness on the street today,
a vehicle screeching into the parking space,
I waited patiently to drive into.
It prowled in the eyes of a clerk behind
the counter, casual in her righteous
bad manners and poor customer service.
Rudeness reappeared on the highway
driving 10 miles under the speed limit
in the fast lane.
It dwelled on the face of my employer
as he voiced his reused expression
"Can't you do anything right?"
Like an old fire hydrant spitting water,
at his adversary, and in the coworker
that keeps pinching my rear as he passes.
The boss that ignores my complaints,
before the "Me Too" movement
was a thang, unaware that a lawsuit
was waiting to happen.

Surfacing again amongst the dirty words,
yelled in my direction, as eyes
crawled across my body,
while strolling past the construction site
of men cheerful in their joking
cause they were only screwing around with me.

Rudeness hovered in the cigarette smoke that
pranced around me, following me,
down the elevator, clinging
to my hair and clothes.
In the market, it appeared comfortable
within the face of a little girl licking
her tongue at me and touching
my white suit with cherry-lollipop fingers,
while mother dear offered no apology.

Later, disrespect showed up as a
big guy with a sourpuss attitude
let the door slam in my face, though I
was only a footstep behind him,
carrying an armload of packages.
Rudeness came decked out in the
enormous hat sitting in the seat
ahead of me in the crowded movie theater.
When I thought I had eluded it,
arrogance resurfaced in a woman screaming,
at the top of her lungs, "Go back to Africa!"
Because I stated I was already waiting
in the line when she stepped ahead of me.

I ran into rudeness on the street today
it approached me in different forms.
Wrapping itself about me, leaping into
my heart and soul.
It's a new tomorrow.
I screeched into the parking space.
The one Karen had been waiting for,
when I decided to pantomime
the responses of others.

Defiant

I bask in the sunlight
and dance in the night.
The challenges you place in my path
cannot outwit me. They give me strength.
I am resistant to your hate.
I've lived with it for a long time.
It has made me defiant against your ugliness.
Your bigotry and the sadness
of your jealousy of our melanin skin.
Pigments that we do not control
Hues that frighten you.
Scared of self-manufactured demons.

I stand with the popular vote
I live among a majority of people
that think like me, feel like me,
and trust in humanity, as I do.
Compassion and caring will defeat you.
I believe.
Pigmentation is not the enemy.
You are.

November 2016

The splintered waves of depression
Silence you in darkness/other times
You scream. You cry.
That happened to me that day
waking up on the morning of
November 9th, 2016.
I was in disbelief, looking
into the TV screen.
Conflicting emotions raged all at once.
As though kicked in the gut/beaten
after a drawn-out battle towards
the voting box culminated with a loss.
Reminded of Ali knocking out Liston.
I was Sonny Liston that dawn
Knocked out by reality.
Thrust into parallelism,
a metaphysical space.
Unaware of the four-year fight ahead
in the universal shift.

Only twenty-four hours before,
confidence in the logical outcome/SHE
would be our next President.
How could a man make fun of a
disabled reporter or brag about
kissing women and grabbing them by the 'P'?

Win?
Crude and erratic behavior is
unaccepted in this country, right?

Not after eight years of dignity, of the first
black family leading the country,
living in a white house built by melanin
bodies. Not after all the votes
he received during his two elections.
Unprepared for the reality check of the new
kleptocracy/and shifting mentalities.
This society elected a sexist/racist
wannabe king into office, leaving the
"Lock her up!" lady by the wayside who
should have been president.
Knowing she was the least
of two evils, knowing none truly worked for me.
Evil won.
Unbeknownst to me, that would be the day
of my four years of verbal/social media
disgruntlement and discontent.
I was angry, but not a dysfunctional angry,
not a dangerous angry. But I was
angrily aware of what was to come.

Tick-Tock

History comes around again,
the civil rights clock rewinds.
Gains to right the injustice of
racism/quickly dissipating as
the hour hand moves backward
ticking minutes to relive the past
as each day breaks from reality
and history reruns to revive
old-fashioned attitudes from
a resentful past.

Snipers have us in their sight,
aiming their destruction/towards
the banishment of our rights.
As history comes around again,
the dominance is clear.
We must be ready for the hatred
that stares us in our faces.
There is no time for waiting,
no twist ending to the dusting
off the hate.
No dancing in the sunset
or butterflies across the sky.
History is a reminder that
time can creep back
into the past.

The present is upon us,
the timer is counting down
the season is now to jointly work
as internal mechanisms move
to swiftly plunge us towards the past,
by lulling us behind the scenes
and trance us back to sleep.
Let's set the pace together.
Let them know today.
We don't punch in on your time clocks.
We'll be the keepers of our time.
The measurers of moments.
The watchers of our ways of life.
We will set the timetable.
There will be no rollback of our lives.

911

911. Call the police.
A black man is standing
down the street.
He's looking at me.
He's staring my way.
My racial anxiety is
high today.
Pull out the phone.
What do you do?
Why are you here?
Just who are you?
Answer me now.
I demand your ID.
This is my neighborhood
You can't pass through me.

Dial 911.
It's a big barbecue!
They're laughing and eating
I think they're intoxicated too!
Your presence is nerve-wracking
you're lingering too long
He's suspect!
He's frightening!
He's strolling past my home.

I'm afraid,
but I'll still follow him
down the street in the dark.

My mask is too tight.
I don't care about rules.
I'll cough in your face
or spit a wad at you.
Watch me run up and slap the
phone out of your hand.
Stand too close, and watch
while I exaggerate my fears
by falling down and crying
white people's tears.
I'll sling poop at your back,
then sic law enforcement on you.
They'll believe when I say
I saw you selling crack too.

Call 911!
Fast-track the law
while I spew racist rantings
of N-word this
and N-word that
back at you!

Because black skin remains
the source of my hostility.
The insults shall continue
as I happily cause you strife
for you having the audacity
to engage in a run-of-the-mill life.

The Passage

Believe that you can,
because you can.
Wisdom of generations
stand ready, stockpiled
to be infused inside of you.
Knowledge prepared to fend off
closed eyes and dead hearts,
those that generate lingering pain.
Descendants
of your descendants
have come face to face
with the burdens in front of you.
The cruelty of man
more powerful than
the kingliest of lions.

Tribes of departed souls
readied to guide your battle.
To speak to you and distill the teachings
of the ancestors.
Listen to the soft murmurs
whispering all around you.
Surrounding and standing by your side.
Armed to aid you on your way.
The forefathers have assembled for you.

Show them respect/be beholden
to the foresight they offer,
the glory of whom you are
who you can be.

Believe in yourself
and the magic and miracles
you can create with a simple touch.
Reach high, higher up, and stretch
your arms deep into the universe
delve farther back into the past
and grab hold of the
wisdom whispers of healing hands.
Extended to facilitate the fight against
negatives of inhumane experiences,
stereotypes and racial tropes.
Strength to encourage the shattering of ceilings
which try to defeat you and
defy who you are,
Children of God.
The rites of passage,
your right to exist.
Bringing to fruition your value
and self-worth.

The kingdom stands beside you,
blood souls buried beneath the soil
of every country, bloodlines
covered by blankets of bounding seas.
To nudge at courage and push you
forward towards hope.
Sealed with hugs of encouragement
to never give up.
Pushing you to believe
that you can because you can.

I Am Not An Inconsequential Word

She breathes a pause.
Sitting in the silence of
speechless space and time.
Contemplating the hurtful comments
hurled in her path, fashioning
her verbal returns to eyes fastened on her,
braced to pounce on her replies.
Those hoping to provoke and break her spirit
hopeful her indignant responses can be
absorbed throughout the air, leaving
only remnants of her dignity scattered
across the floor, waiting for the
'unqualified' label to be employed.
They cling to each move of her body,
each twitch of her eye.
To seize/strike/and scream out,
"Our racist labels apply."

She pushed her pause button, an un-staged
hush, where life, previous/present/future
flashes within seven minutes
to collect thoughts and calm remarks,
as torched fire-breathing whiffs of bias
surround her.
A resonant sigh discharges.
It holds the room's attention,

slipping past the blank minds of the
flame throwers aiming in her direction.

She pauses the gravity of her presence
to stare at the rhetorical assailants,
to strengthen her shield,
steady herself with resolve, and
convey through the silence,
"I am not an inconsequential word."
To be tossed into the world, branded
tantamount to fragmented tattoos.
She remains composed amid the hate.
Her pain kept under control, opting
to cry alone in darkness, still
shedding tears at the rarity of kindness.
Reflections of the noiseless place that I, and
every black woman has tiptoed through.
She took a minute to breathe.
A moment to look back at you.

Face-to-Face with Me

I spoke to my former self today
and revisited the me that I was.
Rooted in deep discussion
over my stumbles and falls.
I met up with my commonsense
where it hid itself then,
and approached the reasons/why?
Not spending the time
to reflect and weave through thoughts
that laid bare the onslaught of pain.
The cause of my lead balloon fails.
Brought to light by the
unsound decisions I made.

I encountered days when I wouldn't
do what I was supposed to do.
Moments when I refused to listen,
ears and eyes barricaded against the truth.
Ignoring the words that edged near to teach
desperate forewarnings of hard days to come.
I reminisced with myself about those
long-gone days to ensure
my continuous journey down
harrowing paths of my life, jogging
my mind, keeping me on track

through the movements
and passage
of each episode of my existence,
evoked by the images
of the moment I awoke,
emerged from broken pieces of me.

Where I learn to love myself
without constraint and
ascend from a history, where I birth
the woman I am now.
Refreshed by my remembrance of
the world spreading itself wide open
to overflow with the sweetness of me.

Jacalyn Eyvonne

I Am Not An Inconsequential Word

Jacalyn Eyvonne

sto·ry

noun

    1. "I awoke to words serenading me in the middle of the night as my story began to harmonize and compose onto a page."

Jacalyn Eyvonne

My Story Continues
Jacalyn Eyvonne

I was the only black student in my class at Gardena Junior High, where I began writing poems, painting, and drawing. Later, I incorporated photography and filmmaking. My art teacher referred to me as a multidimensional creative.

My mother's bookshelves aroused my reading. They covered the entire wall of the den in our household. The shelves overflowed with all genres of reading materials, including the 1969 complete 23-volume set of the Encyclopedia Britannica.

Whenever I opened a volume from the encyclopedia series, I dove deep into an imagination that took me far beyond my south Los Angeles neighborhood. The information contained within the collection was captivating. These books became my go-to texts of knowledge.

Prose, romance novellas, books about history, and magazines co-existed on the library ledges with work by some top thriller and horror writers. My passion for scary stories influenced my compilation "Strange Things Happen at Midnight," a collection of murder, mystery, and short, weird tales.

This sanctuary of information was my favorite place in the house. Likewise, my stepfather's television-viewing man cave was off-limits when he stretched out on his lounge chair smoking his stinky cigars.

The wait did not discourage me as long as I could creep in and pick out a book once he stepped away.

In the 90s, I founded the magazine "In The Company of Poets," afterward producing a local cable access TV series under the same name. I am the founder and director of the Monologues & Poetry International Film Fest and the International KidsNFilm Festival.

Bright Star

I am one among a billion stars.
And yet, the universe has always
spoken to me, though deaf to its whispers.
It wrapped me in cosmic energy,
but I shut it out.
Predisposed to all the things
congesting my existence—the negative words,
the people that hurt.
Absorbing destructive forces
made it harder to change until realizing that I could
activate my story differently and choose the pathway
that would hold me together in a new way.
Today, if I feel without hope for only a moment,
I gaze up into the sky, and I can see myself.

Join My Mailing List

www.JacalynEyvonne.com

Follow on Instagram @jacalyneyvonne

New Collections Coming Soon.

www.ingramcontent.com/pod-product-compliance
Lightning Source LLC
LaVergne TN
LVHW011219080426
835509LV00005B/211